Getting the Message

Getting the Message

The Wisdom of Listening and Thinking

George A. Goens

ROWMAN & LITTLEFIELD
Lanham • Boulder • New York • London

Published by Rowman & Littlefield
An imprint of The Rowman & Littlefield Publishing Group, Inc.
4501 Forbes Boulevard, Suite 200, Lanham, Maryland 20706
www.rowman.com

6 Tinworth Street, London, SE11 5AL, United Kingdom

British Library Cataloguing in Publication Information Available

Library of Congress Cataloging-in-Publication Data Available

Names: Goens, George A., author.
Title: Getting the message : the wisdom of listening and thinking / George A. Goens.
Description: Lanham : Rowman & Littlefield, 2021. | Includes bibliographical
     references and index. | Summary: "This book gives tips on day-to-day
     communication and listening"—Provided by publisher.
Identifiers: LCCN 2020042182 (print) | LCCN 2020042183 (ebook) |
     ISBN 9781475853841 (cloth) | ISBN 9781475853865 (ebook)
Subjects: LCSH: Listening (Philosophy) | Oral communication. | Thought and thinking.
Classification: LCC B105.L54 G64 2021 (print) | LCC B105.L54 (ebook) |
     DDC 302.2/242—dc23
LC record available at https://lccn.loc.gov/2020042182
LC ebook record available at https://lccn.loc.gov/2020042183

FOR

My mother, Stephanie Goens
She taught me to take responsibility and deal with
life's challenges. A real role model.
My father, Earl Goens
He died when I was four years old. I think of him and
miss him to this day. He was never forgotten.
For my uncles, Zig, Bill, and Ed
They each shared a part of themselves with me that is a
part of my life to this day. Thank you.

Contents

Preface

A hawk sat on the birdfeeder at the edge of the open field by the deck. My seven-year-old grandson Eddie was watching, and then the Hawk let out a loud piercing screech, "chwirk." He was fascinated. He asked if birds talk to each other. I said, "Yes, they do."

"But how do they hear? They don't have ears."

"They do, you just don't see them," I replied.

Birds do not have external ear structures, but they do have ear openings beneath their feathers on the sides of their heads. The feathers cover the ear openings to protect them from wind and noise. The communication of birds involves mating calls, defending their territory, finding food, and directing their offspring.

Most animals have means to communicate. Like people, they have different styles of connecting. Most everyone knows that birds sing: some to mark territory and others to raise alarm. Some birds also communicate through their behavior—strutting and dancing to attract other birds. They have needs as other living things do, and they communicate through singing, calls, warbles, and screeches.

I followed up our conversation with, "You know, the question is not whether birds or others can hear, it's whether they really listen! There's a big difference between hearing sound and listening." He gave me a quizzical look.

Human beings have more complex means of communicating: certainly voice, but also physical actions, and also writing, drawing, and other means of expressing feelings and perspectives. While people are unique, they each have similar needs and desires. Any distinction on the basis of heritage, race, gender, or culture does not diminish the essential physiological or emotional needs all people have concerning speaking, being heard and listening.

Being heard goes much deeper than simply hearing one's words. Proper and respectful attention is necessary because people really want to be understood, and words and actions are open to many interpretations.

They obviously engage verbally as evidenced in all kinds of formal or informal situations: caring, loving, directing, instructing, and others. All individuals at one time or another participated in these conversations.

Discussions involve more than verbal exchanges. In these interactions, the parties talk but also communicate nonverbally through physical and facial demeanor and mannerisms, as well as through tone of voice. Verbal and nonverbal expressions should be congruent with the purpose of the presentation, rather than providing mixed messages. But that is not always the case.

Not only is physical action involved in talking and listening, but also there are deeper emotional and intangible issues concerning feelings and relationships. Listening is about sharing oneself through understanding the context and intent of a person's message. Listeners are simply considerate individuals who want to discern another person's thoughts, feelings, experiences, and circumstances.

Communication—talking and listening—takes place at the moment, face-to-face or through online technology. Written notes and letters have a missing link, the physical and immediate presence of the individual, which makes discussions more personal, immediate, and open to greater dialogue. Conversation is distinctive between different people because of the nature of their relationship: formal or informal, family or social, and business or emotional.

Professional discussions generally are more formal in tone and language, in part because of specialized content and organizational decorum. Formality and informality affect discussion, as well as the emotional or cognitive tenor of it. However, the basic quality is to be respectful no matter what the context or content.

Certainly, children have to learn about discussions and how to engage in them. Listening for children is not an easy skill to learn. Actually, it is not simple for some adults either. They get excited, interrupt, and speak loudly or they emotionally shut down. They can be defensive and desire to be "good." Often parents say, "Just listen to me" when having a conversation about behavior as a child tries to justify their conduct or avoid the potential repercussions.

As Abraham Maslow stated: "To be able to listen—really, wholly passively, self-effacingly listen—without presupposing, classifying, improving, controverting, evaluating, approving or disapproving, without dueling with what is being said, without rehearsing the rebuttal in advance, without free-associating to portions of what is being said so that succeeding portions are not heard at all—such listening is rare."[1]

Communication is essential in all facets of life because it concerns not only the physical process of talking and listening but also emotional and psychological concerns and ethics. The nature of the conversation also brings expectations and opens or closes doors to further communication.

NOTE

1. Abraham Maslow, *The Psychology of Science* (New York: Harper and Row, 1996), 96.

Chapter 1

Democracy

The sides are being divided now. It's very obvious. So if you're on the other side of the fence, you're suddenly anti-American. It's breeding fear of being on the wrong side. Democracy is a very fragile thing. You have to take care of democracy. As soon as you stop being responsible to it and allow it to turn into scare tactics, it's no longer democracy, is it? It's something else. It may be an inch away from totalitarianism.

—Sam Shepherd, playwright

It has been said that democracy is the worst form of government except all others that have been tried.

—Winston Churchill

Democracy! It is not easy, and not without disagreement, debate, and divisions. That's just the way it is—and always has been. Democracy is an ideal that requires thought and understanding. However, Winston Churchill was right. It is not without frustration.

Autocratic and dictatorial regimes create social calm and a perverse sense of unity, but they do it through violence and demagoguery resulting in loss of rights—all rights, including free expression. Fear permeates autocracy and individuals are restrained, imprisoned, or killed if they do not abide by directed thought. Communication comes top-down in the form of propaganda. As rights of free speech and expression are eliminated, a counterfeit unity emerges through suppressive and enforced silence.

The United States in its formative documents state clearly in the First Amendment to the Constitution "Congress shall make no law respecting an establishment of religion, or prohibiting the free exercise thereof; or abridging the freedom of speech, or of the press: or the right of people peaceably to assemble, and petition the government for a redress of grievances." Even though it is challenged today, as it has been over the course of history, freedom of speech is a major pillar in American democracy and governance. American character exemplifies a hardworking, independent, and value-based citizenry.

While freedom of speech exists, there is no guarantee of it being heard. Exposure to an audience or the media is not guaranteed. And, even if it were, there is no assurance that people will listen or respond. At times, news stations indicate that those who act and demonstrate for a particular position are representing "the voice of the people." But the voice of the people is not singular: opinions and interpretations come from many sources and directions. Americans speak freely from a number of perspectives. America's voice is multilayered and diverse.

Freedom of speech is essential, but in a democracy, truth is not always easy to discern. A major hurdle is listening: to be not only heard but understood. Media and technology can mask messages' content and focus. Because it is printed and online, it does not mean it is accurately presented and interpreted analytically or objectively.

America's founding documents are based on ideas and principles, not monarchy or autocracy. Those documents uniquely establish a nation based on ideas and the institutional law formulated around them. Expression of the "common" person, not simply the privileged, is at its core through the freedom of the press and public education. Democracy celebrates the "common" person, not aristocracy. Only in America is there a "Fanfare for the Common Man."

Ideas and beliefs are the force uniting individuals of all backgrounds. American citizens are not supposed to be defined by religion, ethnicity, race, or any other demographic. Striving for ideals and values brings people together, although not without debate and confronting change to fulfill the nation's promise. Philosophical principles matter and their implementation raise discourse and controversy. Analyses and perspectives need to be understood and validated, and citizens need to listen and speak out.

The ideas that undergird the Declaration of Independence and the Constitution include liberty, equality, and justice. An essential corollary principle is truth, which is a necessary requirement for citizens to have trust in elected officials or government. Without truth, trust is nonexistent, credibility evaporates, and liberty, equality, and justice are compromised or eradicated.

What makes an American is belief in and commitment to those values stipulated in the founding documents and Supreme Court decisions. The Declaration of Independence cites, "We hold these truths" that "all men are created equal" and have "inalienable rights" including "life, liberty, and happiness." All of these are considerations in determining the goodness and integrity of a society. The concept of justice is a standard in considering whether the ideals of liberty and equality are met.

A civil society is based on meeting those values, which by their openness to interpretation raises the prospect of controversy and dialogue. In this situation, several analyses and actions are presented, and individuals and organizations begin to evaluate and interpret them. The question concerns whether or not disagreements produce reasoned discussions and understanding or simply confusion and arguments.

Democracy requires open and honest communication. Interaction and involvement are necessary. Understanding principles and values and their implication takes not only discourse but also listening. The times change, and the application of established democratic principles can raise questions on such issues as speech, privacy, justice, or equity.

Public debate and civil deliberation on concerns are essential and not about personalities. In politics, however, speaking is given priority because it is viewed as active, and listening is perceived as passive. Power speaks—citizens listen. That is the norm in nondemocratic and totalitarian societies

George Goens, in his book *Civility Lost: The Media, Politics, and Education*, stated, "In reasoned deliberation, individuals and groups are free to choose a course, which requires an understanding of values, the moral implications of options, and the legal authority and correctness of them. This is true whether dealing with personal or societal questions. Responsibilities and duties require moral and ethical considerations and a true understanding of both individual and social issues and their implications."[1]

American society has been harsh online and in social media, demonstrations, and face-to-face circumstances. Categorizing people and making instantaneous judgments build barriers and either silence them or induce reactions of like kind.

Of course, discerning the point of view of others is essential in any discourse. This means listening to and grasping their position and supporting data and facts, and their alternatives and solutions. Too frequently, castigating supersedes understanding without efforts to examine different perspectives and reasoning. Dissent frequently becomes the point, not understanding the scope of the other person's rationale. Debate, however, is not yelling or shouting down. It calls for both a thoughtful interpretation of one's values, as well as the analysis of the viewpoint of others and the values inherent in the issue at hand.

FREEDOM OF SPEECH

Americans speak their minds—to stand up and be counted. Freedom of speech and expression is an essential principle of citizenship in a democracy.

Since citizens are involved in the decision-making structure, they should have voice, although that voice is not always coherent or uniform and, in many circumstances, is in conflict with those in positions of power.

Politicians and elected officials must make sense of the various perspectives and should then decide how to face issues and take action. Citizens hold them accountable by engaging in political debate and expressing themselves, as well when they enter the voting booth.

Conflict, some of it rousing and highly emotional, is emblematic of a democratic republic. While the cacophony of free speech can be confusing and irritating, that is the price of a free and open society. Free speech raises emotions and angers people or motivates them undauntedly to become involved and advocate for their position. Disagreements are expected, and out of them, if confronted properly, can come imaginative and productive solutions. Compromise is certainly a part of the process, as is discussion and active listening.

Values, relationships, and dialogue are the foundation for overcoming differences and bridging divides. Mutual respect allows for respectful differences in politics and encourages understanding of the opinion and welfare of others.

A critical missing link in these circumstances is listening. National documents are silent on it: no statement requires people to listen. Listening is not mandated—it is an assumed responsibility of citizenship. While it is implied with speech and freedom of the press, listening is a central part of citizenship and the decision-making process. However, it is one that is very frequently forgotten, absent, or foreshadowed as people forage for power and authority in the media and the halls of government.

Susan Bickford stated, "Both speaking and listening are central activities of citizenship. Focusing on listening does not require denigrating or diminishing the role of speech, for politics is about the dynamic between the two."[2] She indicates that listening is an important aspect of any adversarial communication because without it, divisions become stronger and deeper, and any sense of understanding and compromise erased.

Unfortunately, in these circumstances, people do not put themselves in the position of other individuals who do not share their perspective. They do not view circumstances from their particular lens and do not try to perceive areas where there are similarities or commonalities. They cannot arrive at a point where they agree to disagree.

This kind of interaction eventually leads to suspicion and fragmentation. People disconnect. Intangibles like trust and respect hold a community and society together, and when they are denigrated or lost, separation occurs. A web of mutual respect and obligation, coupled with shared beliefs and values, lead to connections even if people are not in total agreement on all issues or policies.

Understanding and appreciation of the legal process and established principles provide the basis for community discourse. Agreement on everything is a script for Hollywood movies and not the reality of a true democracy. Differences are inevitable, but they do not have to create fractures or division. Common values open discussion, which can result in finding common ground. However, it is not easy.

Society has, however, become more raucous and self-indulgent and is filled with self-absorption. Individuals throw verbal hand grenades or disparage people's character or stereotype them. Alienation is evident, as people do not simply disagree with others; they express hate and categorize others into "deplorables" and "elites," or bully and name-call—stupid, dumb, crazy, and liars. Epithets are thrown at individuals based on age, gender, race, or other characterizations. All of these divide, raise emotions, and intend to cut off discussion or deliberation. Totalitarian regimes use this approach to disparage people and positions and tear at the fabric of trust.

Hostility toward others can be hateful and bitter. "We Americans are becoming ever better at vilifying people who disagree with us. This taste for hate seems perverse, an intentional pursuit of displeasure. Hate disturbs one's inner peace, as does being hated. But the compensatory pleasures of hatred—in particular its enhancement of self-esteem—are underrated. Hatred is self-congratulatory. It involves expressing superiority to its objects, and patting yourself on the back for not being them."[3]

Hateful expressions destroy any sense of community and illustrate a lack of civility, cognitive understanding, and appreciation of the complexity of problems and possibilities. It is undemocratic and autocratic in tendency and outcomes. One just has to examine the history and the hateful vilification of people and its complicit deranged actions and outcomes to comprehend the slippery slope this behavior leads to.

The breaking of restraints in interactions is, according to Yuval Levin, "the ethic of our age has been aptly called expressive *individualism*. That term suggests not only a desire to pursue one's own path but also a yearning for fulfillment through the definition and articulation of one's own identity. It is a drive both to be more like whatever you already are and also to live in society by fully asserting who you are."[4] As a consequence, individuals release former constraints and express themselves without fear of condemnation or reprisal. Pressure to conform to other requirements and even moral standards is sometimes perceived to impede individuals from "living their own truth," which may not be truth at all.

Hyper individualism is the opposite impulse of "excessive centralization." As individuals loosen the bonds that hold society together, some conclude that control and authority are required to "pick up the slack."[5] Polarization occurs philosophically on both sides of the individualist and collectivist spectrums. Individuals on both ends philosophically disagree on policy and programs, and, unfortunately, the public trust in institutions weakens.

MEDIA AND TECHNOLOGY

American society has moved from broadcasting to narrowcasting through the expansion of technology and the choice it brings. Radio and television technology was dominant in the twentieth century, but that changed to individually controlled and constantly available technology—phones, computers, and iyads. Television, which had four channels, moved to a multitude of choices based on interest, entertainment preferences, philosophy, peer interest, politics, sports, and a whole range of other choices.

In the past, the majority of television watchers would be viewing the same show: for example, "I Love Lucy" in the 1950s had an audience at times of over 70 percent based on Nielsen ratings—71.7 percent of all households with television sets at the time were tuned in to view some programs. Today, characteristically, choice and diversity with Internet services, apps, and a variety of specialties are easily accessible choices.

In the past, newspapers and magazines had political and philosophical slants. Readers could send a letter to voice their position or concern, but there was no guarantee anyone outside the editor would read or see it. Not today! Technology provides easy outlets for voicing opinions and viewpoints, whether they are true or not—instantaneous expression on phones and other Internet applications.

Individuals find respite in their smart phones and preferred sites that echo their political, social, and personal philosophies. People view so-called news programs based on their philosophical dispositions: many only listen to those that promote their viewpoint. Listening to other points of view falls victim to political and technological silos.

Technological echo chambers attract people philosophically and politically who want to hear their own perspective and political disposition repeated and endorsed. Opinions are then perceived to be reality as other positions are mocked or not presented. Individuals do not associate with those outside their perspective, and a sense of the common good cannot be discussed.

When controversies arise, individuals head for their opinion silo, vent, and have their frustration and opinions validated. Sometimes, these silos sow hateful seeds and castigate any opponents as un-American, racist, immoral, communist, perverse, or other epithets. Analysis of viewpoints is not the goal: like-mindedness of thought and perception are.

Silos and echo chambers help destroy the ability for the greater community to engage and converse. It is easier to find endorsement from the silo than engage the larger community with its diverse thoughts, ideas, and people. Silos become safe places for those who are closed to other philosophies or are intolerant of diverse thinking.

Some people find silos comforting because they have a longing to belong, and the larger context could raise personal challenges and conflicts. Finding acceptance with like-minded individuals can be comforting: recognition, not confrontation or opposition, is evident, providing affirmation and connection. The larger context is either not presented or it is consistently refuted. Critical thinking is not always accepted, particularly when it comes to one's own position.

Finding respite in philosophical, political, and other sites protects individuals from hearing, reading, or seeing other viewpoints. True listening is lost in seeking the affirmation of one's beliefs and postures, whether they are true and factual or false and distorted. This behavior turns those who disagree into enemies, not opponents or rivals, closing the door to any discussion or dialogue. Society then becomes splintered, and comments become harsh and often profane—denigrating and winning at all costs is the goal.

John O'Donohue, the poet, stated the issue clearly: "We live in times of constant activity and excitement. The media presents endless images of togetherness, talk shows, and parties. Yet behind all the glossy imagery and activity, there is a haunted lonesomeness at the vacant heart of contemporary life. There is desperate hunger for belonging. People feel isolated and cut off. . . . There is an acute need for the reawakening of the sense of community."[6]

DEMOCRACY AND LISTENING

Government of, by, and for the people is celebrated in every democratic election and in the portrayal of self-government. Unfortunately, listening, as a tool of communication is often ignored and neglected.

Speaking is celebrated. Catchwords, inane slogans, and the search for a Kennedy-esque "asked not" moments are desired. Of course, there is a backdrop of flags and cheering throngs emphasizing all generations, racial and ethnic groups, and genders. In many of these cases, a picture is worth 1,000 words and does not require time or thought. Madison Avenue marketing strategies energetically presenting slogans, thirty-second commercials, and polling, which are used to guide the next series of comments and strategies.

In politics speaking is lauded, along with three-minute television interviews and rehearsed "debate" appearances with the goal of looking presidential, whatever that means. Can you imagine a person like Albert Einstein running for president? Or Eleanor Roosevelt? And, of course, so-called experts, former officials, and other politicians and celebrities interpret remarks and endorse (sell) a particular candidate.

Listening is another side of the political equation. When do the politicians and candidates listen? Is it strictly a one-way street? Are candidates knowledgeable about the position of citizens, or do they simply see the role of citizens to understand their stance as politicians? Is a politician's listening reserved for political advisers, big contributors, or selected influence groups and organizations? The assumption in today's politics is that getting support and votes comes via speaking and media—the portrayal of someone listening is extremely subtle and not very exciting. Politicians frequently feel they have to fill the air with "canned" speeches: listening is not perceived as charismatic.

Do elected officials hear constituents? Polls and data are supposed to provide a "hearing." However, to hear is not synonymous with understanding. Voices are heard and people may agree or disagree on the same things, but the issue is why? Why they hold these views may be for diverse and even contradictory philosophies and reasons.

Understanding why people hold opinions is as important as reporting the views they hold. People may agree or disagree about an issue but have very different reasons and viewpoints as to why. This is significant because why people hold a similar or the same views can be quite different and in itself create conflict. Questions have greater depth than a simple "agree" or "disagree" response on a public opinion survey.

Politicians cannot assume that why people hold a particular position is the same. They can have the same cognitive stance on an issue but have different and sometimes conflicting reasons or values. Informed voters are important, but so are informed candidates who respect citizens and take time to understand their interests.

Listening is an absolute essential in a democracy. Without it, fragmentation occurs, and stereotypes proliferate. Understanding why people hold views is lost. Listening helps identify issues before they become major problems. New ideas and fresh perspectives can surface. An open-ended connection between citizens and officeholders can result. People feel they that they have been heard—and, hopefully, understood.

Politics is competitive and adversarial. Win-or-lose propositions create a contentious, not cooperative, circumstance. This environment causes people not to share ideas or opinions personally to their competitors. Euphemisms are used and specifics avoided. In addition, not everyone is going to agree with what may eventually be determined, but the process of listening, hearing, and consideration is important to acceptance of the decision.

Truly listening and considering what was said takes time. Solving a complex political or economic issue cannot be done quickly or in any helter-skelter manner. Action must be prudent ethically, economically, and socially, and true leaders looking to the common good, and not simply defeating the other party or self-interest.

THE POWER OF LISTENING

Listening is powerful in all venues—politics, work, or relationships. Not listening also sends powerful messages.

In today's politics, there are many examples of leaders and elected officials not listening. In a Quinnipiac 2016 poll, 76 percent of all polled—Republicans and Democrats—agreed with the statement, "Public officials don't care much what people like me think."[7] The fact that members of both parties overwhelmingly support this statement indicates that officials are indifferent to citizens.

Public officials desire and need an audience of citizens and others. Citizens' turning off public officials deprives them of the very thing political figures want and need. A nonresponse is brutal for politicians with all of their planned media and sound bites. In this vein, without citizens listening there can be no commitment or enthusiasm, and without either, the political barometer will not move and elections will be lost.

Elie Wiesel's famous quote is, "The opposite of love is not hate, it's indifference."[8] Wiesel's statement was in reference to people not speaking up in the face of immoral and unethical acts. But it applies to other circumstances as well. In today's political terms, officials need and require an audience to listen. Citizens must not be indifferent to politicians or their proposals because indifference is a detriment to democracy.

Candidates must gain citizen's support. Citizen indifference to officials is not contradictory to the ethical basis of citizenship. Silence in today's politics can be the result of politicians acting on behalf of their own self-interest or special interests. They need votes, and if the public turns them off by not listening, and voting against them, they may wake up.

The power of the "deaf ear"—not listening or responding to them—sends a potent message. Individuals who use speech want recognition and reaction. Sometimes indifference applied in a powerful way against "hate speech" can stifle the publicity and attractions they desire. Responding directly to it usually provides them the attention and recognition they desire and results in more denigrating language.

Standing silent when politicians ask for support is powerful, and it may cause them to step back and examine their behavior or proposals. Silence sends a bigger message at times than directing verbal or written opposition. Silence, followed by action in elections, communicates very dramatically.

Recent elections and poll numbers illustrate that what people tell pollsters does not always match their actions.

When politicians don't listen, commitment evaporates, and they and the government lose the ability to gain credibility and support. The electorate responds by dropping out or mobilizing to make change. Public officials and business leaders require credibility; otherwise, their words become bluster and trite. Huge listening programs are not necessary; sometimes, it comes down to small acts.

The executive assistant knocks on the door and interrupted the school superintendent. "Julia, Mr. Bower is on the phone and wants an appointment with you tomorrow. It's about your funding proposal for school facilities and its tax impact. He sounds very angry."

"I will see him tomorrow at a time that is convenient for him. Book it and modify my schedule if there are any conflicts," Julia said.

The next day, Mr. Bower came and Julia introduced herself and shook his hand. She led him to her office and they sat face-to-face in the comfortable chairs. "Thanks for coming in, Mr. Bower. Would you like coffee or water?"

"No, I'm not here to be entertained. I'm very upset about your tax proposal. People in your job just love to tax-and-spend, and never think of its impact on citizens who don't have kids in school," he shot out.

"Tell me what you think about this proposal and its implementation. I want to hear your perspective and ideas," she said.

"First of all . . . ," The conversation went on for 50 minutes. Most of the time, Mr. Bower talked, gave his views on the proposal, clarified his concerns, and the reason why he wanted to come in and talk about this. Julia asked several times for clarification and perspective. He had specific reasons why he thought the proposal was not the correct path. She listened actively and clarified his ideas and comments.

Then he said, "Well, I didn't really expect this. I give you high marks. I thought you'd give me five minutes and then get rid of me," he said. "You know, I still don't agree with your proposal—I don't buy it. But at least you heard me—I really appreciate that. I hope you consider my position and ideas. I am not alone. And I am not against education. I have to thank you, however, for really listening."

In this case, the meeting did not end in agreement. In relationships, disagreements are not always solved. The issue, though, is how to approach opposition and disagreement.

Political leaders and others can do several things to improve listening and information. Questions can draw people out: "tell me more" or "what brought you to this conclusion?" Paraphrasing a person's position for clarity is also helpful in ensuring total understanding. Clarifying words and their meaning is necessary because differences in age, cultures, and gender have different styles and terminology.

Disagreements can be ideological, sociological, social, religious, or others. Different viewpoints don't have to be uncivil or raucous and they do not mean that individuals cannot get together and communicate respectfully. Working together is not always easy or amicable, but it doesn't have to be hostile. When people disagree, name-calling and categorizing them negatively only create irreparable breaches.

In working with people with different perceptions, a sense of connection has to be developed, in which people listen deeply to each other, explore options, and create new possibilities. This occurs as individuals understand the principles that underwrite the perspective of others. In doing so, they may find that the other person may value the same principles but see their interpretation and application differently. Each party, if they listen, can then better understand the other's interests, as well as grasp in greater depth their own position and approach.

President Barack Obama in a speech in Arizona for the victims of a shooting that included a member of Congress and eighteen others emphasized the need for a fragmented country to come together. He stated, "As we discuss these issues, let each of us do so with a good dose of humility. Rather than pointing fingers or assigning blame, let us use this occasion to expand our moral imaginations, to listen to each other more carefully, to sharpen our instincts for empathy, and remind ourselves of all the ways our hopes and dreams are bound together."[9]

Listening empowers and gives individuals a sense of being respected and recognized, particularly from those who haven't been heard before. Political and other leaders must emphasize listening to better understand citizens and behave in such a way to determine and understand their interests and needs. Listening gets lost in egocentric contexts where bluster and one-upmanship dominates.

Effort is required to listen because the multitudes do not have easy direct access to public officials. While they see polls, those studies provide superficial information—the content and intent of answers may be oversimplified or unclear, plus the structure of the poll can be an issue in terms of phrasing questions appropriately and the scope of people surveyed.

Democracy dies when listening and speaking are curtailed. In fact, some want freedom of speech to be limited, sometimes under the guise of democracy itself. Hearing and voices are lost, and with that listening stops.

Determining that speech should be curtailed, limited, or categorized eliminates the ability of citizens to listen and form opinions and actions. If the government limits or stops free speech, the voice of citizens is diminished and the seeds of autocracy are planted. Free speech and listening go hand-in-hand.

NOTES

1. George A. Goens, *Civility Lost: The Media, Politics, and Education* (Lanham, MD: Rowman and Littlefield), 2019, Loc. 951, Kindle.

2. Susan Bickford, *Dissonance of Democracy* (New York: Cornell University Press, 1996), 4.

3. Crispin Sartwll, "Hatred Enhances Your Self-Esteem," *Walt Street Journal*, July 1, 2019.

4. Yuval Levin, *The Fractured Republic* (New York: Basic Books, 2016), 148.

5. Levin, *The Fractured Republic*, 186.

6. John O'Donohue, *Eternal Echoes* (New York: Cliff Street Books, 1999), 6–7.

7. Quinnipiac University poll, "Deep Dissatisfaction Among U.S. Voters," April 5, 2016, https://poll.qu.edu/national/release-detail?ReleaseID=2340.

8. Ellie Wiesel, "One Must Not Forget," *US News and World Report*, October 27, 1986.

9. Barack Obama, "Remarks: Memorial Speech," https://obamawhitehouse.archives .gov/the-press-office/2011/01/12/remarks-president-barack-obama-memorial-service -victims-shooting-tucson.

Chapter 2

Communication

—The Captain in the movie
Cool Hand Luke

It may be useful to begin to discuss this question by considering the meaning of the word "communication." This is based on the Latin commun and the suffix "ie," which is similar to "fie," in that it means "to make or to do." So one meaning of "to communicate" is "to make something common," i.e. to convey information or knowledge from one person to another in as accurate a way as possible.

—David Bohm, *On Dialog*

Both "Cool Hand" Luke's captain and physicist David Bohm agree that communication must be clear and accurate so it can be interpreted correctly in content and purpose. If it is not, serious or devastating results can occur.

A major catastrophe occurred in 1986 with the space shuttle Challenger, when it exploded after seventy-three seconds into takeoff and resulted in the death of the entire seven-person crew. The Rogers Commission investigating the Challenger disaster stated: "Failures and communication . . . resulted in a decision to launch 51-L based on incomplete and sometimes misleading information, a conflict between engineering data and management judgments, and a NASA management system that permitted internal flight safety problems to bypass key Shuttle managers."

Another spaceflight, the "Columbia" in 2003, disintegrated on entry, killing seven people. In the investigation and analysis, the final evaluation report stated, "Organizational barriers . . . prevented effective communication of critical safety information."

Another communication error resulting in the deaths of 583 people occurred in 1977 because of the miscommunication between the plane's captain and the control tower that caused the crash of two Boeing 747 airplanes. The plane on the ground, waiting for approval to take off, got a message that was misinterpreted by the pilot and he proceeded to take off, at the same time another 747 was landing, resulting in a devastating collision.

Most everyone can cite situations in their families, with friends, and with others that caused strain or difficulties. Examples of poor communication exist in all specters of life.

- Historical examples exist in military ventures that affected the outcomes of battles, the deaths of soldiers by friendly fire, or the death of innocent civilians.
- General Motors had a serious problem with mislabeling an issue with an ignition switch on the GM Cobalt vehicle. The problem with the ignition, which would turn off and deploy the airbags, caused the death of thirteen people. The investigation cited that engineers labeled the ignition switch's problem as a "customer convenience" issue rather than stating it was a major "safety defect."

What is necessary is communication presented in a timely manner with clear language, descriptions, or labels. People must be able to hear or see messages, but they must be timely and clear in the content and intent so that any actions emanating from them are accurate. Obviously, not all misinterpretations are life-ending, but they can create personal hardships and relationship issues. In business cases, loss of trust and financial success is problematic. Words matter.

COMMUNICATION EXPANSION

Human beings need to communicate in all aspects and stages of life. In earlier and simple times, technology or machines were not available to make communication more universal: it was simply face-to-face conversation or the simplicity of pen and paper or through the creative arts. Communication is more expansive today: technology has opened new dimensions and a wider variety of messages.

A broad array of technological innovations is available to the common person to be heard and seen over an expanse of locations and cultures. Contact and connection, however, do not always translate into communication—contact, yes; true connection, not necessarily. A difference exists between them. Connections have a deeper relationship or link: for example, an emotional attachment or a trusting relationship. The contact is an informal acquaintance—individuals known superficially: name, number, and address. Connections, on the other hand, have a sincere bond built on experience and credibility.

The ease of communication does not necessarily improve its quality, demeanor, or honesty. It comes with concerns and problems. Communication styles change with innovation and bring adjustments in people and society.

David Brooks in a New York Times commentary wrote: "When communication styles change, so do people . . . a shift from an oral to a printed culture transformed human consciousness. Once storytelling was a shared experience, with an emphasis on proverb, parable, and myth. With the onset of the printing press it became a private experience, the content of that storytelling more realistic and linear."[1]

Brooks indicates that today's electronic communication emphasizes the pursuit of attention and affection, which used to be private and from family, friends, and neighbors. Electronic attention is wider and more volatile as the search for "likes" becomes more competitive. Today the prostituting of the word "friend" in websites demonstrates that difference. A friend is much more personal and emotionally deeper than a directory of acquaintances.

Problems result. Some individuals seek attention in a number of ways. Some disparage others—narcissism reins and empathy is lost. People put others down, protecting their self-images and lashing out at others. Opinions are celebrated without question and with little or no examination or seeking of truth. Sentiments and passions are stressed. Some seek censorship and restrictions of the free expression of ideas because they find it unsettling emotionally or philosophically. As a result, technology creates silos of thought and orthodoxy leading to compliant conformity. Otherwise people are "unfriended," castigated, or both.

Leon Botstein, president of Bard College, commented that some colleges are hesitant to deviate from "prevailing orthodoxy." He noted, "I think we live in a time when people are extremely intolerant of listening to things they don't agree with. There is the argument that allowing things you don't believe to be said is somehow legitimizing it."[2] He believes that free speech means tolerating disagreeable responses or propositions. A proper response is to take questions and prove the case, not just "shout the person" down. Communication, after all, is two-sided, and how one responds is important.

COMMUNICATION: MORE THAN YOU THINK

Communication includes four basic domains. An obvious one is speaking, which is something everyone does each day about a wide variety of topics and feelings. Obviously, reading is a critical skill, and a major means of expressing personal commentaries via letters, as well as a major conveyor of research, philosophy, legal, religious, economic, and an abundance of other material.

Writing and reading go hand-in-hand and are necessary partners. A variety of writing categories exist—artistic in the forms of poetry, plays, literature, and others—but it also involves documenting information and explanations of research, scientific, social, governmental, legal, or other genres. Expertise is essential in these areas to accurately inform and advise the public or others.

Speaking, writing, and reading need to be understood clearly and correctly, and they require practice and skill. Each is taught in school at all levels because they require different skills. Reading for enjoyment requires a different perspective and skill than reading legal briefs, scientific research, medical documents, or other professional materials. The same is true for writing and speaking. To move into maturity and function as a citizen or in any other adult endeavor, these skills are basic and a part of almost every interaction or employment situation. Writing and reading are dependent on each other as are speaking and listening.

While communication is complex, it does not have to be complicated. The root of communication means to "share" or "to be in relation with." In a sense, it involves bringing people together—speaking and hearing others and sharing ideas and life with them.

Communication is often seen by some as a kind of transportation system—transmitting ideas from one brain to another.

Communication is thus understood as a model of information transportation where we move ideas, like corn in a freight train, from one brain to another. We can hear this idea when we define the Internet as an "information superhighway" or a conversation as an "exchange," or when we describe how advertisements "deliver" messages to audiences and audiences to advertisers. We also participate in the transmission model of communication when we think of education as a process by which teachers "send" ideas out to students, who "receive" them, write them down, and "retain" them. . . . When viewed as a kind of information transfer, communication becomes a merely mechanical routine wherein things like accuracy of the message, the efficiency of delivery, and the precision of reception are in the foreground while other much more interesting and important aspects of communication are missed.[3]

Communication, according to Lipari, is more than remembering and reciting facts and knowledge. In actuality, it brings into view different worlds and perspectives that create new or regenerate relationships, governments, organizations, and law. Different questions are raised, and dreams and ideas are born through dialogue and the exchange of ideas. Insight, foresight, and hindsight emanate from communication if individuals truly listen and think.

Communication is not unidimensional. Generally, the focus is on conversation through the spoken or the written word. However, it is much more—some of it is unspoken and unwritten. It emanates from the arts, which can be more powerful than speeches, debates, conversations, or letters and essays. In totalitarian takeovers, censorship is instituted, and the first people suppressed are writers, poets, artists, and the press. The transmission of ideas is powerful and can enlighten and motivate people.

ARTISTIC EXCHANGES

Artistic forms like music and the visual arts—paintings, sculptures, and photography—have immense power to impact emotion and perspective. When coupled with the spoken or written word, the content and intent of messages are authoritative and influential. Ideas take a stronger form and one's brain is more broadly involved because words, images, and sounds are involved. Complex and critical thinking is required to develop insight.

Music is extremely passionate, and it cogently influences many things tangibly and intangibly. Culture, national identity, and generational links are conveyed in present time or through memories. People connect with lullabies, church bells, or holiday music that frequently trigger memories of the past.

Music throughout our lives brings forth memories and is also a dramatic force for remembering others: loved ones. Old tunes also cause history to come alive complete with its emotion and interactions. Music brings back to life those who died because of the multitiered impact of words, sound, and emotion.

A father, whose daughter died at thirty-four giving birth to his grandson, has flashes of memories of her whenever he hears Aaron Copland's music, particularly *Appalachian Spring*. When she was a teen, he drove her to figure skating lessons three times a week, and they would debate what music they should listen to. She was a fan of contemporary pop music, and he was a jazz and classical music buff. The one piece they both loved was Copland's *Appalachian Spring* that used the Shaker hymn "Simple Gifts." To this day, Copland's music resurrects memories and brings emotion to life of those father and daughter trips to the rink.

In film, music enlivens and provides images emotion, intention, and meaning. A picture may be worth a thousand words, but in film, coupling dialogue and music, emotion is stimulated and deeper understanding of characters and destiny is energized. Spoken dialogue is certainly indispensable, but the musical score provides greater clarity of individual persona and the scene's tone and message.

Film scores like those in *Psycho*, *Star Wars*, *Jaws*, or *The Godfather* bring back feelings and scenes that were preeminent in capturing the essence of the film's story. The music itself brings forth visual recollection and sentiments inherent in those films' written scripts.

In films like *Dunkirk*, which has a limited amount of dialogue, music communicates the significance and mood of the scenes and explains what is occurring and what is at stake. Hans Zimmer[4] wrote the score using music to ratchet up the tension and emotion of the various scenes. In fact, Zimmer used what is called a "shepherds tone" to create the illusion of continuously swelling sound, which repeatedly builds tension and suspense. This musical technique gives the impression of the perpetual rising danger in the scenes documenting the plight of soldiers on the beach, the pilots in the air, and the citizens on the boats daring to rescue the army. Without that score, the film would not have had the intensity and apprehension necessary to highlight the historical significance and the danger and possible tragedy at hand.

In every life experience, sound, sight, emotion, and cognition are involved. Music sets the tone, evokes emotion, creates an atmosphere, and portrays character and attitude. Together, sight and sound unravel a perspective that unites viewers in the experience.

Photographs and visual art are also significant means of communicating images that bring an instantaneous response, whether one of joy, historical significance, humor, or pain. They are clear and simple, highlighting passion and viewpoint, but they are all open to the individual's interpretation of the photographer's intent.

The phrase, "a picture is worth a thousand words" basically means that it conveys complex ideas more clearly and simply than the written word. There can be as much diversity of opinion about a picture as with words. The problem is interpreting the content and intent of the photograph just like with writing or speaking.

With photographs, as with writing and speaking, the photographer's opinion, standpoint, or philosophy has a specific bent or bias. What is left out? What is the story? What is the purpose? What is the tone? A photographer makes editorial decisions on the scene, and the photo sends a message. Whether it is true or not is open for discussion, just as written or spoken descriptions are. When speaking, writing, or photographing, is the whole story presented and is it presented truthfully? Cropping and editing a photograph or picture is no different than revising and deleting written material.

The background, the type of focus, cropping, or view can influence the viewer. Politicians and newspapers are good at this. Various politicians are photographed with a profile of calm deliberation, while others are pictured with their mouths wide open in an unappealing posture or stance. Each perspective delivers a different impression. Pictures and words have an intention. Intent and content are important in interpreting the message, whether it is in film, photos, or visual art.

NONVERBAL COMMUNICATION

The mind and body are not separate entities. Physical behaviors and their expression are often conveyed more quickly than the spoken word. Thoughts and feelings are sometimes transmitted quite spontaneously without the awareness of the person transmitting them. Facial smirks and rolling or squinting eyes communicate very clearly, more so, at times, than speech. Nonverbal communication is irreversible. Once expressed, it cannot be easily modified as the written or spoken word can. Emotional and physical reactions are difficult to edit because they are very responsive to immediate circumstances. And, of course, they are open to interpretation.

Nonverbal reactions communicate many things. Obviously, they express feelings about the verbal message. They also can regulate, control, encourage, or discourage interaction because they can replace words that reinforce or contradict the verbal message.

Blank stares effectively communicate anger, disdain, disgust, or implausibility. A stare with no verbal commentary can curtail further communication. In addition, silence or seeing physical expressions can be powerful expressions of anger or indifference.

Obviously, pictures and images present a nonverbal image and communicate ideas and feelings. Nonverbal communication is prevalent. It conveys whether the person cares, how well they are listening, and whether they believe, trust, or respect the presenter. If those expressions are congruent with what the presenter is communicating, then there is greater trust and stronger connection.

Hands are expressive. A thumbs-up connotes favorability and positive approval. A middle finger salute is a silent indication of disapproval and disgust. Clapping hands gently connotes approval, although they can also communicate sarcasm as faux approval or applause for a modest act. House Speaker Nancy Pelosi's hand clapping at the end of President Trump's 2020 State of the Union message communicated quite a bit without her uttering a sound.

Many speakers use nonverbal gestures: some to punctuate significant points, and others to bring people's attention together. Politicians, religious leaders, children, and others use hand gestures to emphasize and highlight their commentaries. Children with heads cocked left or right and a quizzical expression communicates "who me?" without uttering a word.

Emotions are expressed physically or in prose and language. When children hear a song or a piece of music, they can determine whether it is happy, fearful, passionate, or some other emotion. Composers, writers, artists, and even politicians have an emotional impact on their audience, and music is frequently used in partnership with their communication. For example, when President Barack Obama appeared on stage with his newly elected vice president along with their families, music from the films *Remember the Titans* and *The Patriot* were played. The music coupled with his speech emphasized the spirit and emotion of the historic election and raised feelings and emotions of the viewers and audience.

But there's another aspect. Communicators must be aware of their own emotions because of the impression they have on the nature of their message and its content and delivery. For example, people who are stressed can misread comments and attitudes of others. Knee-jerk responses escalate issues or cause undesired breaches and misunderstandings because of the offensive tone or content.

TECHNOLOGICAL IMPACT

People sitting together in the park, in restaurants, or at family gatherings have phones in their hand and their face on a screen, distracting them from any real cognitive, emotional contact or conversation with others. Technology as destroyed, in many cases, true human connection. Addiction to constantly checking texts, calls, e-mails, or alerts is endemic to younger as well as older generations today. The importance of face-to-face communication is significant and needs to be learned and honored.

Phones and contemporary technology obviously have benefits. Convenience is a major one, but there are also serious downsides—distraction. Whether engaging directly with another person or driving a car, phones can lead to accidents. Always checking one's phone sends a negative nonverbal message to the person they are with that they are not important. The phone becomes more significant than the person in front of them as attention is diverted from a human being to technological device. Experiencing something in person has more power than experiencing it virtually. One's whole body—smell, touch, sight, and hearing—comes alive.

There are even such bizarre innovations as augmented and virtual reality. Are there really technological improvements for true reality? Are the experiences really the same or are there many types of reality? Technological reality falls victim to perspective and interpretation of those creating it.

Actually, there is an irony with technology. Centuries ago, people had to be face-to-face to communicate, and then technology evolved in the form of telegraphs, telephones, radio and television maki contact easier. After computers, the mobile phone transformed into a small device, enabling people to research, call, see, hear, email, and contact people—all in one simple device. Today, people text rather than call and converse. Texting is nothing more than a technological telegram, except people do not have to write "stop" at the end of sentences.

Today's generation, the IGen born between 1995 and 2012, is the first to grow up with smartphones as a constant part of their life from the very beginning. They hit the market in 2007. Obviously, parents, teachers, and others have concern over screen time, but there are other issues related to phone use by adolescents.

While not the sole cause, the rates of teen depression have increased since 2011. In addition, many screen activities are linked to unhappiness. In an article in *The Atlantic Magazine*, Jean Twenge[5] states that eighth graders who spend ten or more hours a week on social media are 56 percent more likely to say they are unhappy than those who spend less time.

The National Cancer Institute on Drug Abuse has conducted a Monitoring the Future Survey of 12th graders since 1975 and 10th graders since 1991. The survey reports about how much leisure time is spent on non-screen time (social interaction and exercise) and on-screen time (texting and social media). "Teens who spend more time than average on-screen activities are more likely to be unhappy, and those who spend more time than average on non-screen activities are more likely to be happy. . . . All screen activities are linked to less happiness, and all non-screen activities are linked to more happiness."[6]

The bottom line is that adolescents—and probably adults too—should "put down the phone, turn off the laptop, and do something—anything—that does not involve a screen."[7] The more time adolescents spent on-screen time, the more likely they are to report symptoms of depression. Phones do not provide comfort: people, particularly parents, do.

Phones and screen time isolate people from direct human contact, and that can make them feel remote and left out. Face-to-face conscious contact and communication with others are tangible expressions of acceptance and interdependence. For those in teen years, being a part of a peer group is important; friendship is more then texting.

Some IGen and Millennials are so addicted they sleep with their phones. It is the last thing they see each day and the first thing they see when they awake. The constant use of phones in bed can cause a shortage of sleep, affecting concentration and attention.

Texting can be easily misinterpreted because the content may be clear, but the intent could be seriously misinterpreted. "Nice going!" could be a compliment or a sarcastic epithet.

Cell phones can be distracting not only in impersonal interactions but also in other social situations, work, or school. According to a PEW research study, adults indicated it is inappropriate to use cell phones in the following circumstances: at a restaurant (62 percent), family dinners (88 percent), meetings (94 percent), and ritual services (96 percent).[8]

Mobile phones affect creating positive human relationships. "Evidence . . . indicates that the mere presence of mobile phones has inhibited the development of interpersonal closeness and trust, and reduced the extent to which individuals felt empathy and understanding."[9] The effect of mobile phones was most pronounced if individuals were discussing issues of personal meaning to them, beyond usual casual conversation.

Today, there is concern for isolation and loneliness by people of all age groups. Technology can constrain personal engagement and true communication. As comedian George Carlin stated, "Remember to spend some time with your loved ones, because they are not going to be around forever."[10] Having a friend, colleague, or family member by one's side and peering into the screen of a phone and ignoring them is a grave mistake and a waste of the limited time people have on the planet.

COMMUNICATION FOCUS

Why people communicate is more diverse than simply updating what happened in one's life. The focus can be much greater. Communication is self-revealing: who one is, what they stand for, what they are feeling, what ideas and thoughts they have, and what they need.

In many cases, simply providing information and sharing stories, events, gossip, or other things is common. Friends engage in this "small talk" frequently, providing impressions and opinions about the world and mutual interests.

Emotions are frequently the purpose of communicating. Feelings can be positive or negative and can self-disclose attitudes and perspectives about life. Emotions and feelings are about affect more than hard data, facts, or experiences and often expressed through body language.

People also have imaginations and share stories, jokes, and personal points of view. Some of these messages are intended to entertain, both from serious or humorous perspectives. Imaginative communication is the core of books, magazines, films, plays, and conversations that moves into many creative realms.

Business, politics, and enterprise focus on persuasion. Influencing the beliefs, postures, and actions of others takes place in the workplace as well as in families. Today people are inundated with advertising trying to sway them and the general public about goods, services, and materials. Persuasion also extends to personal relationships, as well as raising children.

Ritualistic communication exists in religious and public ceremonies where individuals are expected to perform in certain ways individually and collectively. It is intended to unite people in common recognition or celebration of values, institutions, or a way of life.

Communication of these types takes place in a variety of ways. As humorous as it sounds, individuals do talk—communicate—to themselves. They speak to themselves as they ponder issues or contemplate situations. Thinking internally about situations and direction is actually essential to finding options and making good decisions.

Other types of correspondence take place interpersonally, one-to-one, which occurs every day and in many circumstances. In addition, small groups engage in social, business, educational, or other conversations. People who are employed also confront organizational communication, which is a more formal system of interaction and exchange of ideas.

In entertainment, politics, and government, communication is generally a one-way process with two roles: speakers or presenters and listeners or viewers. An explicit purpose is the goal and communication approaches are specifically organized to augment and focus the message. Media are involved in many cases. Communication requires planning and coordination particularly to ensure clarity and consistency of the message.

COMMUNICATION ISSUES

When people are not happy with outcomes, communication is often cited as the culprit. It is often the "canary in the coal mine." This simply means that other issues may be the real concern, but the global term communication covers almost everything from workload to relationships to compensation to evaluations to any number of things.

Communication, however, can be a problem—a serious one that deflates relationships creates conflict, and handicaps productive behavior. The issue regularly concerns failure to listen accurately. Interruptions and distracting behavior result in individuals not feeling heard, understood, or respected.

At times, people discuss issues from different philosophical, cultural, or role perspectives that lead to misinterpretation and misunderstandings. People talk over each other and make assumptions about others that lead to conflict or a lack of concern—they don't listen.

Misunderstandings are going to take place. People with varied histories, philosophies, or cultures interpret issues differently, and explanations and conclusions can be misunderstood. The circumstances can open individuals to listen more closely and to see their differences and review and possibly renew their own perspectives. They might even lead to understanding through greater patience. Others, without a broader perspective and empathy, may not question the issues, but simply blow up the conversation.

Ego and attitude are major roadblocks to discourse. A superiority attitude or "know it all" perspective restricts conversation and deflects any personal relationship from developing. Not many people want to create a relationship with arrogant or superior ego-maniacs. Ego desires continual acknowledgment and recognition. Ego frequently concerns defensiveness and aggressiveness to promote the image of competence, intelligence, and power.

People believe nonverbal communication more than verbal. For example, with lying behavior, several positives are displayed:

- Awkward pauses in conversation
- Higher pitched voice
- Deliberate pronunciation and articulation of words
- Reduced eye contact
- Increased delay in response to questions
- Increased body movements, for example, changes in posture
- Business communication decreased smiling and rate of speech[11]

Another major issue is communication that is poorly thought-out. Rants are not convincing. Profanity denigrates the conversation, and jargon or pretentious language disconnects people. Pretentious language or sloganeering eliminates any serious or thoughtful consideration of what people want to express. What people say or write, and how they do it either contributes to the success of their message or can be the foundation for their failure.

Communication is intended to connect with other human beings. In many cases, the objective is noble and expected to make things better. When people hide behind the veneer of arrogance and ego, there are usually other issues and fears at play.

Compassion is necessary for communication to truly understand the person's total message. Peter Drucker, management consultant and author, stated, "The most important thing in communication is hearing what isn't said." In a sense, reading between the lines is necessary to fully comprehend the purpose and objective of any communication. Words and how they are presented—tone, inflection, and manner—must be interpreted correctly to understand the substance and emotions of the message.

NOTES

1. Brooks, David. "When Trolls and Crybullies Rule the Earth," *New York Times*, May 5, 2019.

2. Akst, Daniel. "The Reopening of the Liberal Mind," *Wall Street Journal*, May 24, 2019. https://www.wsj.com/articles/the-reopening-of-the-liberal-mind-11558732547

3. Lipari, Lisbeth, *Listening, Thinking, Being* (University Park, Pennsylvania: Pennsylvania State University Press, 2014), 10.

4. "Christopher Nolan Explains the Audio Illusion that Created the Unique Music in Dunkirk," *Business Insider*, July 24, 2017.

5. Jean M. Twenge, "Have Smartphones Destroyed a Generation?" *The Atlantic*, September 2017, https://www.theatlantic.com/magazine/archive/2017/09/has-the-smartphone-destroyed-a-generation/534198/.

6. Twenge, "Have Smartphones Destroyed a Generation?"

7. Twenge, "Have Smartphones Destroyed a Generation?"

8. Andrew Perrin, *PEW Research Center*, "10 Facts about Smart Phones as the iPhone Turns 10," June 28, 2017, https://www.pewresearch.org/fact-tank/2017/06/28/10-facts-about-smartphones/.

9. Andrew K. Prysbylski and Netta Weinstein, "Can You Connect with Me Now? How the Presence of Mobile Communication Technology Influences Face-to-Face Conversation Quality," *Journal of Social and Personal Relationships*, July 19, 2012.

10. George Carlin, "Something to Ponder," *The Medium*, January 1, 2018, https://medium.com/@johnhubertz/note-i-have-requested-carlin-family-permission-to-republish-this-brief-essay-but-have-not-received-4b59003c36ce.

11. University of Minnesota Library, "Business Communication for Success," 2015, https://www.lib.umn.edu/publishing.

Chapter 3

Ethics

There may be times when we are powerless to prevent injustice, but there must never be a time when we fail to protest.

—Elie Wiesel

Restriction of free thought and free speech is the most dangerous of all subversions. It is an un-American act that could easily defeat us.

—Supreme Court Justice William O. Douglas

As John Dewey once said, "Society exists . . . in communication." Living in harmony with oneself and others requires open-minded communication. Emotion is housed in words, expressions, and phrases: philosophy and ethics are the foundation on which they stand. Courage is required to express standards and to be self-revealing and ethical in communicating.

Without open and ethical communication, positive relationships would not be possible at home, work, or in society. Sharing and exchanging ideas can raise people's hopes, create understanding and rally people around principles and ideals, which move people far beyond simply providing information.

Democracies will, by their very nature, have differences of opinion and raucous times. To expect otherwise is an indication that individuals do not truly understand a free society. Communication unites or divides and has always been and remains controversial today. Philosophies clash and raise concerns about the direction of actions and proposals. Free speech and press are the portals through which ideas and viewpoints are expressed.

Goethe stated, "wisdom is found in truth." Truth, however, is not always easily discerned and is a major responsibility for listeners. Critical, but civil, thinking is necessary. In democracies, speech in all its forms is intended influence, but it also is the path to discern fact from fiction.

Philosophy involves knowledge and thinking, reasoning and wisdom. Rational or critical thinking is more than beliefs because of the reliance on reasoned investigation and proof. Reflection on nature and values is fundamental in determining goodness and wisdom based on moral and ethical standards. Values, ideas, and principles are a vital part of philosophical positions and judgments.

Citizens need the ability to analyze issues and make an argument on all sides of a position. In that way, people fully understand the questions and arguments at stake. Doing so is essential in all aspects of life, and certainly in understanding ethical positions and one's rights as a citizen.

Making an argument or taking a position involves the capacity to think through issues and, understandably, express oneself in speech, writing, and other means of communication. Understanding means that a person comprehends the upsides and the downsides (strengths and weaknesses) of their position or argument as well as the opposing viewpoints. Rhetorical skill in any format demands knowing the audience and mastering oratorical skills, writing, and presentation to be effective. Clarity is a major requirement, so people understand the complete message and the tenor of its presentation.

RESPONSIBILITY AND ETHICS

Ethical standards are critical to ensuring the freedom to communicate appropriately to assure that an audience will listen. Degrading others is a sure way to lose an audience. In discussions, ethics and values are frequently a concern. Emotions drive people's conduct, which create ethical implications for both the speaker and the listener.

Ethics in interpersonal communication involves the intention of content and how it is presented. Individual choices are involved. Openness to others and respect for their position, feelings, and values, as well as communicating accurately, are critically important.

A major challenge is discerning the position of others, even if disagreement seems imminent. Deception and ambiguity serve no purpose if the expectation is to create open discussion and an exchange of views. Respect, not agreement, is a major quality of conversation and exchange. Comments such as "I don't agree with your position on this, but I appreciate how you presented it."

Respect for the audience, whether it is one person or a multitude of people, is a major ethical concern. Individuals should be viewed as possessing dignity and worth. They are significant even if they do not agree philosophically or pragmatically with their advocated position. Respecting ideas coming from the audience is important.

Name-calling or terse quips like "get over it" or "that's _ _ _ _ist" terminates any prospect of dialogue, stops listening, and curtails any possibility of mutual understanding. Speakers must value freedom of expression and tolerance for diverse ideas and viewpoints from their audience just as they desire it when they deliver a message.

In addition, speakers must understand the consequences of their message and review how they present it. Will it stimulate or curtail thoughts and relationships? Will it create breaches that are destructive and irresponsible? Does it degrade whole sectors of society? Should people respond in the same disparaging language of others? Will it result in indifference and apathy?

Ethical communication requires several qualities. First, it must be truthful, factual, and honest. Second, content must be applied clearly and professionally. Finally, the speaker must understand the information, facts, and data, and present them clearly, accurately, and without distortion.

In a very simple way, it boils down to basic things. First, even with individuals who hold opposite views, respect is necessary. Without this quality, attentiveness is lost and nonverbal behavior becomes indifferent and inconsiderate. Individuals should respect others, and listening is a primary indicator of respect.

Second, pre-judging a speaker betrays being open to what the individual thinks. Listening first is the ethical thing to do before drawing conclusions. If there is a disagreement at least respecting individuals' right to speak opens the possibility for other discussions.

Even if one disagrees with the speaker's content, there is also the opportunity to connect personally with the individual and, possibly, even become friends or colleagues. Friendship does not depend on always thinking the same philosophically or procedurally. In fact, open discussions and debates are often the basis for friendship.

Finally, being open to free expression is a value that demonstrates civility for both the individual and the nature of a democratic society itself. Ethically, open expression cannot be reserved for a few and then restricted for others. Free expression is not limited to just those with a majority opinion. Hearing all sides may produce new ideas and perspectives that enhance the probability of success. People with fixed mindsets are not open to unfamiliar and different approaches.

TRUTHFULNESS

Ethics and communication relate to "goodness" because it concerns truthfulness. There is a critical difference between knowingly distorting the truth—intentionally misleading others—and unknowingly expressing a false-hood. Deception occurs because of bias, misrepresentation, slander, or dishonesty. Intentionally misleading others is unethical and totally unprofessional.

The major challenge for the listener is to discern whether the comments or presentation is truthful. Any semblance of deviation from the truth, simply put, expands and places into question the entire presentation. Small errors or untruths lead to serious reactions and lack of trust. Questioning to clarify statements and propositions is important for all listeners, as well as for the presenter.

Truth in communication simply means that one does not lie: knowingly telling a fabrication. To garner respect and confidence, truth is necessary. Otherwise, trust is lost, and when that occurs, credibility is destroyed along with honor and credence. Being forthright and honest are the foundations for respect and reputation. Being labeled a shill, liar, or fabricator is a disaster for anyone who wants to contribute to any genuine discourse professionally or personally.

To communicate ethically, honesty is fundamental and at the core for responsible and thoughtful decision-making. Decisions have implications, both short and long term. Consequences are endemic to decision-making and the communication that goes into their determination. Hence, truth matters—GIGO is at play if communication is manipulative, misleading, or consciously distorted. GIGO means "garbage in, garbage out." Knowingly falsifying or using questionable, or erroneous information or data renders bogus conclusions and consequences—and it is unethical.

How to behave in raising and pursuing a discussion concerns the formal and informal aspects of the relationship. Are they individuals?, Colleagues? Rivals? Experts? Subordinates? Advisers? Acquaintances?

WHAT TRUTH?

Today, we often hear the phrase "speak your truth." This phrase raises a question about whether or not people are actually speaking in a factual sense, or are they simply providing their impression and opinion on matters. What a person feels and thinks may be their belief, but not the actual truth. In a court of law, there is no place for "one's truth," only the truth.

If someone was to talk about their life and how they got to where they are today, that is one thing: sharing their journey to becoming the person they are. But if speaking "your truth" involves a perspective that does not match with facts or research, then using the term "truth" is incorrect.

Opinion is a better descriptor. While respecting a person's opinion is appropriate. Truth is erroneous unless justified by facts and research, and not just a point of view. There are opinions, but there is no such thing as "my truth." What matters are scientific, legal, historical and financial, or other verified facts.

Individuals assess the accuracy and helpfulness of communications, as well as the manner in which they are offered. People can be seen as clear, thorough, and concise, or just covering up for his or her boss or saying what needs to be said. Any one of these phrases draws a conclusion about the character of the person personally and professionally.

Communication confronts several issues: the relationship between speaker and listener, and the purpose of that relationship. Relationships have ethical aspects to them, some concerning when and how communication takes place. How to respond is dependent, not only on those aspects but also on the time and imperative of when and how decisions are made. Motives and relationships matter because it is a two-way process.

Not presenting available information also can place the listener in a precarious position. Standing silent when alarm is apparent to others is unprincipled and unethical. The communicator has an ethical responsibility to ensure truth for the security of others and themselves. The message and the manner it is communicated must be ethical because it is a matter of personal and professional character and honesty.

Communication involves judgments about ethics and standards of behavior. Standards such as "honesty, promise keeping, truthfulness, fairness, and humaneness usually are used in making ethical judgments of rightness and wrongness in human behavior."[1]

Too often statistics and polls are used and data are not reported fully, accurately, or properly. In many cases, the conclusions may not be correct or valid. Data sometimes is culled and handpicked by the presenter to support a particular point of view, and the data that does not is ignored. In addition, sample sizes or other research design issues may not be appropriate for the data to be valid. Data must be timely to the issue and not out of date. Obviously, data and information should never be falsified, manipulated, or plagiarized. However, many people perceive statistics as proof of truthfulness because they appear scientific. Numbers can be wrong depending on their pertinence, validity, application, as well as how they are collected and interpreted.

Duties, obligations, and principles are important aspects of communication. In formal settings, like journalism, they direct decisions about gathering information and determining whether or not to present it and how and when it should be relayed. Reputations policies or procedures, some with moral consequences, are involved.

Truthfulness, accuracy, objectivity, impartiality, and fairness, along with "imitation of harm," protecting minor children and others are important considerations. Unanticipated consequences exist in all decisions, but if there are matters of ethics and harm, forethought and safety are integral to professional conduct.

Trust and truth go hand-in-hand. To some, "white lies" seem harmless because individuals don't want to hurt another person's feelings about their personal choices of clothing, hairstyles, and others. So the easy way out is to simply agree with them, rather than criticize their personal taste and choices.

Lies are not harmless. In business, politics, or families, they bring large consequences and affect how people live and work together. Lies encourage deception as well as manipulation. Relationships in all domains are based on confidence, care, and credibility, all of which are necessary for people to have faith in each other and their character and work. In marriage, for example, lies destroy the foundation of love and values that brought two people together. Once breached it is extremely difficult to resurrect, if at all.

In face-to-face communication, the subject of lying comes up. Telling the truth is an absolute. But others would argue that the ends justify the means. Is it ever ethical to lie? Circumstances may create a situation where the moral thing to do is to lie. For example, in totalitarian governments, as history has demonstrated, some members of the population are disparaged, incarcerated, or killed because of their ethnicity, race, opinion, politics, or other factors. By answering questions truthfully, lives could be jeopardized and ended. By being truthful one can be an accomplice to violence or immoral policies and actions.

If an individual is questioned about a person or family in this context, should the person questioned tell the truth? Here the ends may justify the means—withholding the truth and engaging in a lie may be the moral thing to do. However, there may be personal consequences if individuals are caught in their deceit to power. History has compelling examples of this dilemma. Deception in this case may save lives, but it can jeopardize one's own, as well as others.

These issues are heart wrenching and morally complicated. Conflicts between two or more values or principles can occur, which raises very difficult concerns. Do some values supersede others and then be compromised? How does one justify that decision? Historically, people confronted choices that cost some lives in order to save many others. Military decisions have had to be made on this premise. Conscience takes a toll and, as seen in military and other circumstances, can result in psychological repercussions or other issues.

Deception and lies in other situations simply get in the way or deflect responsibility, destroying one's character and reputation. In judicial hearings, there can be severe legal consequences. In employment, individuals can lose their jobs, and the company or organization can face severe legal and other repercussions if misinformation, fabrications, or falsehoods are used. Discerning between lying and interpreting or perceiving things differently is a difficult issue as many court cases demonstrate.

Ethics involves values and principles. Preserving life supersedes truth in a deprived and immoral personal, political, or social environment. Acting in a virtuous manner can be complicated, raising issues of what is just and morally correct. Are some virtues more important than others?

LEADERSHIP AND INTEGRITY

A number of leaders erroneously think that they have to act and speak in a certain way in order to gain support and stature. However, leaders come in all shapes and sizes, genders and races, and philosophy and goals, and they all have one primary goal: they want people to listen and to follow them.

What causes people to want to follow a person and their leadership? Basically, it rests on integrity, which is recognized when people see leaders consistently acting in ways that are consistent with their promises and values. Integrity relies on a series of actions, not just one, and builds over time.

While consistent behavior is important to integrity, it can be destroyed by one action, decision, or proposal. Leaders with integrity are consistent in addressing their philosophy and processes, as well as being transparent and demonstrating self-control. Too often, leaders, particularly those in politics, offer grand solutions, without ever discussing the positives and potential negative outcomes of their own proposals. Presenting one side of an argument, indicates ignorance of the total consequences of the proposal or fear of presenting potential questions or problems. Either way, leaders damage their standing.

Leaders with integrity have an understanding of their personal limits. Caricatures in movies and literature often paint leaders with tremendous insight, ability to rouse individuals to a cause and to overcome victoriously with total support for their victory. Fiction may be comforting, but in reality, victories may also result in criticism and uncertainty. There are times when the interpretation of values and principles differ, and results may include other complications that people want to avoid.

Why do people want to lead? That question addresses not only the mission of the organization but also the interior motives of the person seeking to lead. The mission or goal of both must be ethical and moral.

History has clearly defined individuals who had the skills to be leaders, but who did so for corrupt and immoral purposes. Some for self-interest and others for purposes that were morally corrupt. Every century has examples of unprincipled individuals or movements that had degenerate, depraved, and unprincipled motives and outcomes.

True commitment of people comes from a sense of integrity and belief in the mission of the organization and its leaders. If leaders are egregious to employees and the public, the organization will fail despite its honorable purpose.

People require a sense of dignity and self-worth in order to fully commit to a cause. Poor leadership can be a cancer that destroys trust and, eventually, the organization. A leader's true power and influence is based on relationships that have a foundation on ethical values and principles. Then, others will pursue positive outcomes on a foundation of trust.

THE ETHICS OF NOT THINKING

Communication spurs thinking and thought—that's why some want to control and censor it. Truth is different from opinion or dogma, and various people and organizations do not want some viewpoints expressed. Questioning and raising issues are what freedom of speech produces: contrary to totalitarian regimes, there is no thought control.

Hannah Arendt discussed the focus of totalitarian governments. "The ideal subject of totalitarian rule is not the convinced Nazi or the convinced Communist, but people for whom the distinction between fact and fiction (i.e., the reality of experience) and the distinction between true and false (i.e., the standards of thought) no longer exist."[2]

American values and principles of free speech actually create conflict and ire. Political and social issues are complex and open to any number of interpretations. Contemporary society is diverse, which raises issues in communication. Bringing people together and communicating in a diverse society requires an understanding of democratic principles and possibly finding common ground around them.

Communication is supposed to be a pathway to truth. The truth raises controversy and conflict. Albert Camus, the French Nobel prize winner, stated, "Seeking what is true is not seeking what is desirable."[3] Sometimes, the truth hurts.

Autocrats and dictators restrain information and the media by controlling or restricting speech and free expression—to stop free expression of thought and exploration of the truth. Oppression in speech is done through propaganda or censorship, control of the press and universities, and, in some cases, physical repression. In a free society, citizens must be educated in order to discern truth from falsities and propaganda. Education is an essential need for citizens to be able to function in a free society to ensure that the government does not have direct and total control of their lives.

Citizens have a responsibility to ensure that rights are preserved and enforced to make certain that society maintains and enforces the rights of free speech and communication. Discussions and explorations of what is and what is not true must continue in debate and dialogue. Discovering the truth affects perspective and stimulates possible options, both positive and negative.

Aristotle stated, "It is absurd to hold that a man should be ashamed of an inability to defend himself with his limbs, but not ashamed of an inability to defend himself with speech and reason; for the use of rational speech is more distinctive of a human being than the use of his limbs."[4]

Certainly, government and political propaganda can be rampant creating doubt in the minds of citizens, and opening the door to fear and mistrust. Campaigns of mass persuasion use emotion and selected data to move people to behave in a particular way, sometimes beyond reason. One just has to examine corporate and political marketing campaigns to realize that reason is not always the main focus—passion, selling, and branding are. The whole truth may not be the focus, nor is providing complete information. In these cases, the pursuit of power corrupts.

Arendt discussed politics and truth. She stated, "Factual truths are never compellingly true. The historian knows how vulnerable is the whole texture of facts in which we spend our daily life; it is always in danger of being perforated by single lies or torn to shreds by the organized lying of groups, nations, or classes, or denied and distorted, often carefully covered up by reams of falsehoods or simply allowed to fall into oblivion. Facts need testimony to be remembered and trustworthy witnesses to be established in order to find a secure dwelling place in the domain of human affairs."[5]

For individuals, ethics must move beyond getting promotions and financial rewards. Deception or distortion of facts to promote their positions and opinions is not acceptable. In addition, they should not engage in conflicts of interest and recuse themselves from engaging in communications and conversations for their own benefit.

In summary, preparation to fully understand issues, positions, and personalities is important. Being honest and respectful, and not using abrasive language and name-calling are important to build relationships that are open to ideas and discussion. These are necessary for civility and respectful relationships to develop and endure.

FREE SPEECH

Free speech includes artists of all stripes, poets, music, writers, and others who are free to express their ideas, creativity, and opinions. It also protects picketing, parades, flag and cross-burning, armbands and demonstrations. To many, they may be offensive or off-limits to their interpretation of American values and patriotism.

The First Amendment states: "Congress shall make no law . . . abridging the freedom of speech or press." Government under this amendment has no authority or power to restrict free expression because of its message, ideas, subject matter, or content.

Basically, the amendment calls for tolerance. Tolerance because it "presupposes that the freedom to speak one's mind is not only an aspect of individual liberty—and thus a good unto itself—but also is essential to the common quest for truth and the vitality of a society as a whole."[6] There are a few limitations.

In order for citizens to listen, they have to hear or read opinions, essays, or other means of exercising speech. If that is restricted or censored, then the ability to listen to and contemplate ideas is compromised. Free speech and the ability to be heard are representative of a democratic republic. Without it, indoctrination arises as autocracies dictate what can be heard, seen, or read—limitations imposed by those in power in order to keep it.

History has many examples of speech, debate, and dialogue being curtailed, based falsely on maintaining a civil society and political power. Issues of restraining free speech come from both liberal and conservative sources. There can be highly extreme repercussions.

Book burnings, blacklisting books, or the removal of them from libraries are a characteristic of these efforts. In addition, it seeps into education by controlling the content of school textbooks and curriculum. Indoctrination and spewing a regime's mantra is not education, and it stops the flow of ideas and complex thinking. Journalists become restricted and, in some cases, imprisoned.

Speakers at some universities have been restricted and require police protection because of their philosophy or subject matter content. These examples alone certify the importance of free speech and its power.

Today, as has happened in the past, free speech is an issue. The concept of "hate speech" has been used to restrict speech, articles, books, and online postings. Free speech, however, raises debate and sometimes incivility and emotions and hurt feelings can erupt. People become angry, and former conflicts and turmoil are reborn.

According to proponents, besides being offensive, "hate speech" can be emotionally damaging and socially marginalizing. Speech labeled as "hate speech" includes epithets and prejudicial statements based on race, religion, ethnicity, disability, and gender. Is labeling a person a racist or Nazi hate speech under this position? In addition, some even go so far as believing that speech should not be offensive or insulting. Humor and satire could come under this category. Who would determine what is offensive or insulting is not cited. Being ignorant and offensive is not against the law and is open to individual interpretations of perspectives.

Speech cannot be punished if it is hateful, according to Nadine Strossen, former President of the American Civil Liberties Union, "Although the Supreme Court has never recognized a special category of 'hate speech' that is excluded from First Amendment protection based on its message alone, government may restrict some speech with a hateful, discriminatory message (as well as speech that conveys other messages) if, in context, it directly causes specific imminent serious harm, thus satisfying the emergency test."[7] Strossen indicates that responding in-kind to hateful speech and censoring them is the wrong approach to curtailing it.[8] These responses only initiate stronger rebuffs and greater exposure.

Comments by Chief Justice John Roberts of the Supreme Court illustrate the nation's commitment to free speech in order to protect and maintain, not stifle, public debate. "Speech is power. It can stir people to action; move them to tears of both joy and sorrow, and. . . . Inflict great pain. On the facts before us, we cannot react to that pain by punishing the speaker. As a nation we have chosen a different course—to protect even hurtful speech on public issues to ensure we do not stifle public debate."[9]

The US Supreme Court has consistently rejected to prevent or punish "hate speech." Decisions were made on the basis of Justice Oliver Wendell Holmes 1929 statement to guarantee the "freedom for the thought we hate."[10] The rationale is that it is dangerous to discourage thought and imagination and to breed the possibility of fear and repression, which in turn leads to hate and separation—all of which impairs and endangers the stability of a democratic government. The idea is that reason can defeat negative or hateful propositions, while reducing the freedom of expression will only enable nondemocratic propositions.

Confidence in an elected citizenry is reflected in law. A democracy is not a place safe from being challenged intellectually and emotionally with ideas—some thoughtful and honorable and others brash and hateful.

The power of reason is critically important in a democracy. Discussion and civil debate, along with clarity of rationale and intention, can lead to defining the solutions to issues and problems. Mark Twain provided a perspective that should be considered. He stated, "Anger is an acid that can do more to the vessel in which it is stored than to anything on which it is poured."

Free speech is a critically important principle in a democracy, as well as in relationships. Free speech is not an absolute, and it involves ethics as well as a designated freedom in the First Amendment. Speech can produce negative responses and castigation and can encourage censorship, all of which have ethical as well as legal implications. Name-calling and stereotypes are aimed at restricting speech through unethical depictions and caricatures that represent people in negative ways morally or politically.

These depictions are negative and intended to scare the other person without making a specific case and are intended to damage without presenting facts or evidence. Political parties have engaged in this behavior. Today's technology makes it very easy to post a comment or position resorting to these strategies. Truth is not always a principle in these cases; however, creating an image is.

In a presidential election, the term "deplorables" was used as a descriptor for some citizens. Is being peacefully deplorable unconstitutional? Labeling individuals as racists, fascists, communists, terrorists, socialists, or traitors are efforts at character assassination. Mudslinging, unfortunately with the rise of technology, has become more common. With free speech, some individuals express despicable attitudes toward others. Is the solution censorship?

Historically, people's reputations and livelihood have been severely damaged: Senator Joseph McCarthy in the early 1950s is an infamous example, when he alleged without evidence that some people were communists. In some cases, this accusation cost people their livelihood. Both parties and others today have used empty accusations as a political tool.

Successful liars can convince themselves of their own lies. The self-deception exists socially, as well as in government and other realms of life. It can be destructive to both the individual and their reputation personally and professionally. Self-deception should not exist in government or any other social agency like newspapers and media.

The Free Press is an extremely important protector of holding government and others responsible for truth. The Pentagon Papers about the Vietnam War is a prime example of the value of the free press.

The First Amendment presumes that government is a servant of the people and that free speech leads to the truth. Speech, however, is not unlimited. John Stuart Mill expressed a "harm principle," which states in his essay "On Liberty": "All that makes existence valuable to anyone depends on the enforcement of restraints upon the actions of other people. Some rules of conduct, therefore, must be imposed—by law in the first place, and by opinion on many things which are not fit subjects for the operation of the law."[11]

Under this premise, the ideas of privacy, security, and democratic equality, and the prevention of harm are considerations. As in the classic example, yelling "fire" in a crowded theater is not allowed. Defamation, perjury, incitement to lawless action, solicitation to commit crimes, child pornography, and blackmail are some categories the First Amendment does not protect.

Noam Chomsky commented, "If you are in favor of freedom of speech, that means you're in favor of speech precisely for views you despise."[12] Free speech creates conflict and can be unsettling, but under principle, it allows the chance of determining the truth rather than having a government official or others determine what citizens can see or hear. The court system and the

Supreme Court are the main arbitrators of speech. In a free society, citizens must be educated in order to discern truth from propaganda and falsities.

At universities today, debate about speech and speakers exists as individuals want "hateful" speech suppressed and speakers denied the opportunity to express their positions. In the past and at times today, political conservatives wanted some speech suppressed, for example, McCarthyism is a prime example. Today, liberal activists want certain speech to be eliminated and have used shaming and ostracism as a tool.

Supreme Court Justice Benjamin Cardozo declared that freedom of speech "is the matrix, the indispensable condition of nearly every other form of freedom."[13] Debate presently exists about speech—whether it is hateful or harmful, and whether it should be controlled. Cardozo clearly specifies that freedom of speech affects almost all other freedoms Americans have.

If certain types of speech are not suppressed, and people find it offensive, what is the alternative to its suppression? The "Supreme Court has held strongly to the view that our nation believes in the public exchange of ideas and open debate, that the response to offensive speech is to speak in response."[14]

Supreme Court Justice Louis D. Brandeis stated, "If there be time to expose through discussion the falsehood and fallacies, to avert the evil by the processes of education, the remedy to be applied is more speech, not enforced silence."[15]

Ethics and standards protect people, not from hearing distasteful things but providing them the ability to respond through their own freedom of speech. Citizens with freedom of speech have the right to respond as long as violence is not proposed as a solution. Free speech allows individuals to counter ideas and positions that are in opposition to American principles and beliefs. Political and other speech is necessary for democracy to thrive, but civility is an important aspect of social and other dialogue.

Personal and professional ethics and principles are the foundation pillars for relationships and responsibilities. Ethics raises issues and controversies based on their interpretation and application. Understandably, continually reviewing the application of ethics and values as society changes and innovates is an ongoing and necessary discussion and debate.

NOTES

1. Richard L. Johannsen, Kathleen S. Valde, and Karen E. Whedbee, *Ethics in Human Communication* (Waveland Press, Inc., 2007), 1, Kindle.

2. Hannah Arendt, *The Origins of Totalitarianism* (Harvest Books, 1973), 474, Kindle.

3. Maria Popova, "Albert Camus on Consciousness and the Lacuna Between Truth and Meaning," *Brain Pickings*, https://www.brainpickings.org/2016/12/26/albert-camus-myth-of-sisyphus-consciousness/.

4. Edith Hall, *Aristotle's Way: How Ancient Wisdom Can Change Your Life* (Penguin Publishing Group, 2019), 77, Kindle.

5. Hanna Arendt, *Crises of the Republic: Lying in Politics; Civil Disobedience; Nonviolence; Thoughts on Politics and Revolution* (Houghton Mifflin Harcourt), 6, Kindle.

6. John Paul Stevens, "The Freedom of Speech," *Yale Law School*, October 27, 1993.

7. Nadine Strossen, *HATE: Why We Should Resist It with Free Speech, Not Censorship (Inalienable Rights)* (Oxford University Press, 2018), xxxi, Kindle.

8. NPR, "It's Been a Minute With Sam Saunders," Free Speech vs. Hate Speech, https://www.npr.org/templates/transcript/transcript.php?storyId=616085863.

9. US Supreme Court, Snyder v. Philips et al. October Term, 2010, https://www.supremecourt.gov/opinions/10pdf/09-751.pdf.

10. "Hate Speech," *The Fire*, March 29, 2019, https://thefire.org/issues/hate-speech/.

11. John Stewart Mill, "On Liberty," *Stanford Encyclopedia of Philosophy*, https://plato.stanford.edu/entries/mill/.

12. "Ethics Explainer: Freedom of Speech," *The Ethics Centre*, February 22, 2017, https://ethics.org.au/ethics-explainer-freedom-of-speech/.

13. Stephen Wermiel, "The Ongoing Challenge to Define Free Speech," *American Bar Association*, https://www.americanbar.org/groups/crsj/publications/human_rights_magazine_home/the-ongoing-challenge-to-define-free-speech/the-ongoing-challenge-to-define-free-speech/.

14. Wermiel, "The Ongoing Challenge to Define Free Speech."

15. Thomas Healy, "Whose Afraid of Free Speech?" *The Atlantic*, June 2017.

Chapter 4

Listening

Courage is what it takes to stand up and speak out; courage is also what it takes to sit down and listen.

—Winston Churchill

Wisdom is the reward you get for a lifetime of listening when you would have rather talked.

—Mark Twain

Listening is complex, requiring concentration and understanding. Nonverbal actions, including thinking, memory, and emotion, are involved. Hearing, seeing, and physical expression and actions are also involved, as are tone and touch. From a physical and mental standpoint, a lot is happening. Interpreting, comprehending, and responding, both nonverbally and verbally, provide feedback to the speaker about how accurately and well the message was received.

Listening is not always easy. Society can be cacophonous. Individuals seek solitude and quiet moments away from its clamor. Technology, however, is everywhere—TVs blaring and canned music playing in elevators, hallways, doctors' offices, stores, and almost everywhere. While all intended to entice people to relax or buy, they are distracting.

Luke and Betsy met at a coffee shop to catch up on their lives and work. Eighteen months passed since they last saw each other. They were anxious to listen to each other's exploits, but hearing got in their way.

The coffee shop, Marty's, had a very pleasant environment with artwork from local artists decorating the walls, comfortable seating, and friendly staff. Light jazz played on speakers quietly in the background as people sat by themselves or with friends or family.

The found a table for two and listened to each other's humorous and serious antidotes. At one point as Betsy commented about her father's health, at the same point the barista turned on the bean grinder that startled Luke ["What the heck was that?" he thought as he glanced over to the counter]. He looked back as she continued talking. Two men at the table behind them burst out laughing, and raised their voices about the incredulous circumstances in their families ["Cripes, these guys are irritating. Keep it down," Betsy thought.]. Shortly after, a fire engine drove by siren blazing and honking traffic out of its way. [Both looked out the window.]

All the noise interrupted their focus, along with the dissonance of talk, brewing machines, soprano saxophone's playing over the speakers, and muddled conversations. In addition, the colorful paintings and the smells of roasted coffee and baked goods, as well as the comfortable ambience of the shop affected Luke and Betsy's focus. Luke was mesmerized by an abstract painting of sunrise.

Cheryl, the manager, alleviated their discomfort and found a quiet corner of the shop with a small table and comfortable chairs. She said, "Sorry for the distraction, Betsy. It gets very busy and noisy this time of day. How about another cup of coffee on the house?"

While talking and listening, a multitude of sensations affect concentration and conversation. Individuals' inner thoughts, feelings, and emotions are invisible forces that call for attention. Minds wander unintentionally.

Obviously, hearing affects the ability to listen; people must hear the person with whom they are talking but also be in a setting where they can hear clearly. The vibrations of the surrounding environment can seize attention and focus. Distraction of all types curtails true listening.

Listening involves focusing on the speaker and paying full attention to the words and concepts while eliminating the other sensations that compete for attention. Thoughts and perceptions can easily divert and disrupt concentration.

Listening is an absolute necessity to connect with another person and succeed in all relationships. Skillful listening is the bridge for genuine connection with others in all aspects of relationships. Without it, communication is hampered and understanding lost.

Listening is actually the first communication skill learned in the development of a child, and the one used most in the course of a human life: 46 percent of the time communicating is spent listening. Speaking is next, applied 30 percent of the time, while reading and writing are used 15 percent and 9 percent, respectively, in a person's lifetime.

Ironically, speaking, reading, and writing are taught in schools to a far larger degree than is listening, which in some cases is an assumed skill because people are able to hear.[1] Hearing and listening are not synonymous, as everyone has experienced at times. Listening is wrongly perceived as easy—simply hear the words and reply. Hence, speaking takes prominence over listening.

The assumption is that because listening is the first skill young children demonstrate it comes naturally. Babies hear sounds without any formal training. Seeing them respond to voice and, eventually, commands and expressions assume that listening just evolves without any formal training. It simply is thought of as a matter of being quiet and exhibiting good manners.

People presume that because individuals hear someone and understand their words that they are truly listening. But it takes more than that. Listening entails thinking, comprehension, and understanding, in addition to considering the nonverbal communication that is taking place simultaneously. Interpreting both verbal and nonverbal expressions requires deep attention to grasp the story and ideas, coupled with feeling, heart, and mind.

Listening is a part of being with others in the world and has ethical implications.

Most people think it is simply about conversation, but listening to another person gives them a voice—being heard respectfully as a human being.

Everyone has desires, fears, ambitions, and dreams. To have them truly heard involves risking being open and trusting others. Struggle is a part of life. If people are truly heard, both the speaker and listener realize that they are connected. Words and feelings unite people around common needs in life's journey.

WHY LISTEN?

Listening has several important purposes. When uncertainty exists about what a person feels or thinks listening is the great clarifier, because at times the person's talk or physical impressions are not clear. Active listening can help clarify issues for both of these, and other listening strategies can build a bond between individuals—caring and truly understanding build trust.

In situations when people get upset—for known or unknown reasons—listening helps them lessen their anxiety and assists them in confronting their issues. These situations require, in many cases, simple listening so that individuals can consider their feelings and circumstances. The listener is not there to solve problems: simply to listen and understand, which are important because they are indicators of caring.

Certainly, interpersonal communication is dominant. Family members, spouses, friends, and a multitude of others engage with each other and require conscious listening. The workplace and social situations press for listening because results emerge from clarifying missions and problems, along with the ability to possibly brainstorm and consider new ideas.

The nature of these conversations is a factor in why and how one listens. Interpersonal conversations and routine personal matters and schedules are one thing—"Do you think we should go to dinner with Emerson?," is one simple conversation. But there are others, which go far beyond into deep feelings and thoughts

In another discussion, the person stated, "What are the legal restraints of pursuing this idea and proposal?" Here, clear understanding of issues and consequences requires analytical thinking to determine appropriate recourse. A greater depth of knowledge, thinking, and listening is required—more analytical and speculative. Listening and communication are certainly more complex than just determining if and when going to dinner with "Emerson" is going to happen.

The manner of listening depends on the nature of the interaction. The conversation can be strategic or political in which "listening in" is important to comprehend the circumstances but also pushes individuals out of just understanding the message to actively presenting new insight and ideas. Listening opens fresh perspectives and ideas about relationships or life's path, because it enlarges the envelope of experience, knowledge, and attitude.

Theoretical conversations are not easy and involve a give-and-take between people trying to discern truth. In these sessions, minds may not meet or agree. Often more than one discussion is required and, in fact, may continue without any final conclusion. However, these conversations help individuals to clarify an approach or create greater understanding in order to proceed with conditions and approaches.

Sometimes, simply broadening and creating a deeper understanding and perspective are important outcomes so that progress and innovation can advance. Listening stimulates individuals to come together and commit, which involves far more than simply keeping quiet. The impression often is that if the person is sitting quietly that they are listening. That is not necessarily the case.

At one time or another, most everyone has experienced individuals who give the perception they are listening, but they are not. Pseudo-listening is a label for individuals who appear to be involved in the conversation but, in actuality, are ignoring or only partially listening. Sometimes they engage in this because of some other personal need that supersedes any communication with others, making the conversation insincere and, to use a harsher word, bogus.

People engage in pseudo-listening for different reasons. Some are simple, like forming responses instead of focusing on what is said, being preoccupied because there is too much on the individual's mind, lack of familiarity with the topic, social pressure to participate in the conversation, or uninterested but trying to be polite.

The demeanor of the speaker also contributes to this issue; if they lack self-confidence, nervousness, and other personal can distract participants. An individual's mind may wander; they may be examining the person's mannerisms or their physical characteristics rather than listening to his or her words. At other times, the speaker's phrases or comments initiate an internal emotional response that causes listeners to shut down and negate anything else they have to say. Certainly, lack of interest or boredom with the subject generates a respectful quiet and no response.

Daydreaming silences any words, sentences, or paragraphs—they are not heard or comprehended. Daydreaming is not an unknown entity to many students in regard to lectures or to citizens concerning political or other speeches and discussions. Desiring to be somewhere else initiates active thinking about other people, places or things.

Listening and reading require a similar process. As Mortimer Adler states, "In both, the mind of the receiver—the reader or listener—must somehow penetrate through the words used to the thought that lies behind them. The impediments that language places in the way of understanding must be overcome. The vocabulary of the speaker or writer is seldom if ever identical with the vocabulary of the listener or reader. The latter must always make the effort to get at a meaning that can be expressed in different sets of words."[2] Siphoning out the meaning of the speaker regardless of how they verbally express their message or put their sentences together is at the core of comprehending content and its interpretation.

People get sidetracked by how individuals express themselves—tone, physical actions, volume, humor, etc.—and tune out their message. For example, the mayor said, "We have a serious peristeronic problem in this city." A citizen, Callan, was thinking, "What kind of problem?" Using obscure terminology is "for the birds," as they say. In this case, that is correct in more ways than one because the peristeronic concerns pigeons. Without truly listening and understanding the person's main points and position, one cannot determine whether they agree or disagree. How else can the expertise of a person be determined?

Listening is a pathway to discerning the meaning and validity of speech and comments, which involves assessing the main ideas and conclusions, and whether they are based on thoughtful arguments and factual evidence. Determining whether conclusions are sound and the consequences reasonable should be clear. Unfortunately, many political speeches geared to persuasion fall short because they do not highlight a comprehensive analysis of plans or proposals. They are simply one-sided assertions.

A major issue in any conversation is respect, which requires releasing ego or other personal needs in order to be fully affected by the speaker. Ego can turn off openness and comprehension of the person's philosophical, intellectual, and emotional position. Letting go of any ego needs or predispositions or prejudgments is necessary in order to truly listen; otherwise, minds are closed.

Focusing and listening to another person is a gift of consideration, patience and civility and being fully present physically and mentally to the speaker. Total focus is an indication of respect, and with respect understanding develops and increases. Both of them can grow and change as a consequence of this relationship.

LISTENING AND SELF-UNDERSTANDING

In conversations, the question frequently arises, "Who is this person?" Not their name, title, or position, but who they are as an individual—their personal qualities and motivations. What people bring to conversations is their inner self and their experience, attitudes, beliefs, and values. All affect the nature and content of relationships and communication.

People will sometimes say as a negative impression, "He really has an attitude!" Attitudes are brought to conversations: they are learned predispositions or demeanor that people acquire through their life experience. They affect references and points of view.

Beliefs and values can evolve with time and experience. Convictions guide an individual's conduct and attitudes. As people mature and learn, some long-held beliefs may change—sometimes positively or negatively. Beliefs develop from prior experience or education and provide a frame of reference for their perspectives and attitudes.

Values are at the core of one's self-image and behavior and define issues as good or bad, or right or wrong. Values can change over a lifespan, through a major life-altering event or maturation and learning. Values influence interactions (belonging and support), promotion (success and power) norms for behavior (obedience), excitement (emotion and pleasure), actualization (knowledge and maturity) and existence (health and stability). The strength of those values varies at different stages of life and emotional experience. Values are the basis for self-direction, creativity, leadership, and persistence.

Listening plays a part in helping people through difficult times of loss, illness, or confusion. In these situations, people need a listener: not someone to offer solutions or physical assistance, just someone to listen quietly with a sense of deep humanity and consideration for the other person. Sitting silently with a person in grief communicates concern and sympathy. Listening intently can simply provide comfort to another person facing emotional or other challenges.

People need to have their fear, grief, or despair heard. Presence is helpful and is a sign of love and care. Listening to what hurts or is troublesome can help a person face some of the darker moments of life. This requires a listener to empty oneself to allow another's story to enter, opening to the energetic movement of emotion, empathetically joining with someone else's experience."[3]

Sometimes people need to feel and listen to their own heartfelt feelings and communication and determine what life is asking of them. In addition, by listening and reflecting about oneself, people can come to grips with failure, success, and pain.

Eric Fromm defined the rules for the art of unselfish understanding that have implications for listening. The basic rule for practicing this art is the complete concentration of the listener. Nothing of importance must be on his mind, he must be optimally free from anxiety as well as from greed. He must possess a freely-working imagination which is sufficiently concrete to be expressed in words. He must be endowed with a capacity for empathy with another person and strong enough to feel the experience of the other as if it were his own. The condition for such empathy is a crucial facet of the capacity for love. To understand another means to love him—not in the erotic sense but in the sense of reaching out to him and of overcoming the fear of losing oneself. Understanding and loving are inseparable. If they are separate, it is a cerebral process and the door to essential understanding remains closed.[4]

In this process, self-knowledge is necessary because emotions can intrude and damage listening in serious discussions and personal connections between people. Narcissism destroys connection and trust, and an intellectual conversation will be halted as a consequence. In heart-to-heart conversations, emotion is going to be present, but in other kinds of discourse—theoretical or impersonal—emotion can stymie any two-way interaction. People turn off and stop interacting because of discomfort or if anger is apparent.

REFLECTIVE LISTENING

First of all, knowing the purpose of the conversation is necessary. At times, individuals do not have a clear perspective on why it is taking place. This in itself creates confusion and leads to misunderstanding of the reason for getting together.

Listeners acknowledge speakers by stating in their own words the content of the person's message. Understanding the information and data is important, as is realizing the person's feelings and attitudes.

Summarizing is an effective tool by the listener to help the speaker perceive whether or not the message was heard and understood clearly. At times, the content is understood, but the intent is not. Intent concerns the meaning of the message—sometimes, positive words are expressed in the veil of sarcasm or anger. Emotion provides the intention of words and statements.

Another issue is the context of the conversation, which impacts purpose and understanding. The environment and moment must be appropriate: not all venues are the right place for business, personal, or difficult conversations. For example, the local coffee shop may not be the best place to discuss a critically important legal problem. Time and place are relevant to the nature of the message.

Critical thinkers should be able to discern truth from propaganda. Propaganda is intended to achieve the specific and desired intent of the communicator and is not neutral or objectively presented. It is designed to promote a partisan cause or ideology. Propaganda raises the issue of communication ethics and values. Unbiased information is shared in order to better understand the world, society, or circumstances, and not push people to a particular point of view.

To determine whether or not there is agreement on content requires focused listening and thoughtful silence. Clarifying words and terms is necessary because they can have different significance or inflection. Determining the intent and definition is essential. Clarifying is a very important skill listeners need.

Several types of talk are evident between individuals. An obvious one is social conversation, which takes place in coffee shops, neighborhoods, social gatherings, and almost everywhere where people connect and engage. These conversations do not necessarily result in conclusions or decisions, but may simply be about "catching up" on the lives and dealings of individuals.

In this conversation, several things may be avoided that can stop the interaction. Conceit, name-dropping, vulgarity and slurs, and prying into the personal life of the other person are destructive. Any one of these will terminate the discourse. Gossip and digressing into tangents are also conversation killers, along with excessive jargon or unnecessary academic parlance.

Personal conversations about family or relationships are far deeper than business or academic talk. Husbands and wives engage in this kind of dialogue and, if they don't, they will soon be headed for divorce court. Heart-to-heart discussions are essential, as each person understands the feelings and status of their relationships, connections, and lives—otherwise, the bond between them can break. People need others with whom they can confide safely and confidentially.

Silence between husband and wife can fracture the communion of hearts and minds. It can be a more severe transgression than saying harsh things because it declares, in a way, indifference. Not saying a word rips the attachment between people and leaves little hope of resurrecting sensitivity and compassion. Again, not being heard leaves a void, and any heartfelt connection is difficult, if not possible. Conversely, so often husbands or wives will say that their spouse "truly understands who I am like no one else in the world." Acceptance and empathy are a part of true love.

LISTENING: TYPES

Andrew Dobson, in his book, *Listening for Democracy*, stated, "Listening is a planned and deliberate act in which the listener is fully present and actively engages the client in a nonjudgmental and accepting manner."[5] He highlights the necessity to understand and appreciate the individual's perception and story, which requires empathy to comprehend the obvious and underlying meanings.

Dobson identifies several types of listening[6] One type is compassionate listening, in which listeners divest themselves of their personal thoughts, judgments, and feelings to offer "hospitality" to another's pain and feelings. This person provides space for the other individual to be heard.

Cataphatic listening is the total opposite of compassionate listening, which basically is not listening attentively but is simply organizing responses. Cataphatic listening is close to not comprehending. This type of so-called listening will not lead to a deep understanding or dialogue. Sometimes, ego drives this form of listening.

Aprophatic listening can, according to Dobson, produce dynamic dialogue that is associated with political life. This type of listening involves "opening the self to the other and holding one's own categories in abeyance."[7] In this way, the speaker's voice can be heard authentically, and the listener can process what was heard by asking questions for clarification and making sense of the communication.

In aprophatic listening, the other person's perspective, frame of reference, and their emotions are understood. The aprophatic listener avoids interjecting and being a "know it all." Listening here means understanding through empathy and compassion a person's victories and their defeats and viewpoints. Positive connections between the speaker and listener can be made.

Another form of political listening is forced listening, which is as negative as forcing someone to do something they do not want to do. Being a captive audience and facing propaganda blasts is devastating to any meaningful connection. People in business, families, or politics are often caught as part of a captive audience: lack of pertinence destroys any intent to listen.

LEADERSHIP AND LISTENING

Anyone working with people as a colleague or leader has to have a respectful and trustworthy relationship. Leaders, in particular, need refined listening skills because they spend over 70 percent of their time communicating with colleagues, teams, and others, including policy boards and community.

People often consider leadership as telling people what they should do: directing and controlling. The nature of a crisis may require quick and decisive action to save lives, respond to tragedy, or deal with immoral or unethical conduct. Policy matters and deliberation, however, require reasoned thought and listening to bring people together.

Today, the complexity of issues and the pressure of time, telling and commanding are not always the answer. Sometimes issues have to gestate or need time to completely unfold. Space and time can be valuable, rather than rushing to judgment. In crisis situations, direction is necessary for safety and relief, understanding that in these circumstances all information may not be available and will require more comprehensive answers and solutions.

But with long-term planning, immediate direction is not always the answer because all points of view are necessary, and thinking through the consequences of each is an important requirement.

Communication is an integral part of leadership. People will not easily rally around a policy, plan, or direction without honest and straightforward communication. In that sense, leaders must engage in two-way communication: telling is not sufficient, nor is it always an indication of leadership or leader behavior. People differ in their emotional orientations. Good leaders understand this and use a variety of means to communicate and listen. They understand that symbols communicate very powerful messages.

Leaders communicate in the way they act. Nonverbal communication is symbolic: how they carry themselves, interpret and relate are powerful. Messages come in many forms, including nonverbally. Individuals can see— physically—whether the person is sincere and speaking from the heart or is simply reading a statement and doing business. Facial expressions and tone of voice are important reflections of attitude and feelings.

An open mind is needed for leading a family or any organization. Autocratic approaches squash openness. Colleagues and employees shut down because "Why should I say anything, they don't listen anyway!" Autocratic approaches destroy openness, consequently, so people do not share issues and problems, as well as perspectives and prospective solutions. Leaders have an obligation to ensure organizational values are upheld and provide support and motivation, as well as encourage creativity from committees and teams.

Openness to listening and discussion provides leaders and colleagues with insight into what issues are surfacing and the opportunity to be proactive, not reactive. Listening leads to greater understanding and improved analyses and better decisions. The organization and leaders learn and determine a hard truth and are then able to objectively adapt.

Respecting the arguments of others in a civil manner is a major leadership act. Arrogance is repulsive and breaks relationships. Disrespect alienates individuals and destroys any effort to unite people's efforts. Overemotional tirades stop any interaction or listening on the part of others. If the leader does not have personal or professional integrity, statements will fall on deaf ears. Without trust, emotion, and reason people will not follow them.

Open-mindedness offers colleagues and others the ability to share new ideas or remodel old ones. If there is disagreement, it must be done respectfully, allowing others to be able to express their position and or question new propositions so that the best answer or approach can be refined or selected.

Leaders must recognize that everything is not about them. They must continue to learn and sense that the best sources for information and concepts may be citizens and employees. Humility matters because leaders do not know everything. Respecting the intelligence of others is invaluable to the leaders and for success, and recognizing the contributions of people brings rewards and creativity because they feel valued and find meaning in their work.

Being comfortable in their shoes and not play-acting as a leader demonstrates genuine mindfulness. Sincerity and understanding ensure that a leader really listens and is cognizant of both what is said and what is modeled.

A leader should be an "idea person" looking for better ways, exposing and correcting weaknesses and problems, and demonstrating interest in what others think. They are clarifiers and analyzers with the help of others. Leadership dies if only "yes" people are hired. Those who challenge ideas intelligently are staples of a vibrant organization, and challenging the leader's position should not be off limits.

Leaders and others must genuinely show people that they care and are valuable assets who are cared for at work. An empathetic leader makes an intangible connection and demonstrates concern for people at all levels of the organization or team.

Organizations benefit when people are loyal and committed. Relationships are strengthened when leaders listen and teamwork increases. Good leaders are credible in their listening, understanding, and trusting because they realize what is at stake for the organization, as well as for those who work for it. People have voice when the leader listens, and together they can determine a shared truth and move ahead toward larger objectives.

RULES FOR CONVERSATION

Occasionally, some people have no idea why they are involved in the conversation taking place or its purpose: Providing information? Brainstorming? Debating? Defining implications?

Particularly in serious circumstances, the right people with the right background have to be at the table. In this vein, the issues at stake require discussion and exploration from the participants. This is true in crisis or emergency situations.

The other issue concerning listening is to ensure everyone has their say, not just pushing one's thoughts and agenda without understanding the viewpoint of others. Conversations get diverted if people do not understand the questions or perspectives others have.

Framing questions clearly so they can be understood are prerequisites. In any conversation, talking and getting no response is running into the proverbial brick wall and is frustrating. The listener could be at fault by interrupting or distracting others by smirking or other nonverbal actions to discount the speaker's credibility.

The behavior of speakers can curtail the success of having people listen. The focus of the conversation can be thrown off by some sophomoric or vacuous behavior. Examples include egocentric talk, whining—which is annoying and purposeless—and redundant droning or over-killing a point or idea, all of which result in audience frustration and disconnection. Wandering all over the intellectual map is a turnoff—getting to the point clearly and quickly is fundamental. Irrelevant stories are sideshows and taxing. Speakers who interrupt others and cut them off demonstrate insensitivity and lose the respect of the audience. Some speakers belittle the audience and arrogantly pontificate on their ignorance and lack of intellect.

Speakers have to be aware of their audience. People have differences in philosophy and values, and society is much more diverse. This includes race, gender, or cultural diversity. In society, businesses, or other sectors, individuals often cling to like-minded individuals who share their perspective.

Having a solid background and expertise are basic for speakers: they must know what they are talking about and have a significant message. Passion about the subject is powerful and is strong and intense with deep feeling and emotion. Powerful experiences and stories activate audiences, producing more personal connection and understanding.

People seek answers and understanding of issues. Being negative is tiresome. Complaining and the constant reiteration of shortcomings or failures are not going to capture people's attention or imagination. This happens frequently, unfortunately, in politics. Just criticizing a politician or persistently dispelling a program or policy without offering a clear-cut direction turns people off. They want a positive recourse to issues, not just negative diatribes or trite name-calling.

When people listen, the speaker must remember that the audience might have comments or suggestions. Listeners and speakers are not metaphorical sponges—they can respond to ideas and solutions and, in doing so, clarify the thinking and positions of others. Both can build on their interactions by keeping an open mind and being attentive. Clarification between each is important for responding and feedback given with care is helpful. Humility for both listeners and speakers is indispensable to build a positive, caring connection. Respect emerges from these relationships.

Listening builds a sense of community much more so than speaking. When people listen to one another, they become one, bound together and offering their valuable time. Really listening is powerful and moves beyond simple categorization and certainty of ideas and positions and illustrates that everyone together lives in a shared world. "Perhaps it might be something like *listening being*, where when you are listening, really listening as opposed to hearing or interpreting, *you are* that listening, such that listening constitutes the very being of your being. Listening is what we are: *Homo audiens*, listening being."[8]

NOTES

1. Mortimer J. Adler, *How to Speak—How to Listen* (Touchstone, 1997), 89, Kindle.

2. Adler, *How to Speak—How to Listen*, 91.

3. Miriam Greenspan, *Healing Through the Dark Emotions* (Boston: Shambala Publications, 2003), 15.

4. Erich Fromm, *The Art of Listening* (Open Road Media, 2013), 192–93, Kindle.

5. Andrew Dobson, *Listening for Democracy* (Oxford University Press, 2014), 50.

6. Dobson, *Listening for Democracy*, 64–68.

7. Dobson, *Listening for Democracy*, 70.

8. Lisbeth Lipari, *Listening, Thinking, Being* (University Park, Pennsylvania: Pennsylvania State University Press, 2014), 102.

Chapter 5

Voice

You never really understand another person until you consider things from his point of view—until you climb inside his skin and walk around in it.

—Harper Lee, *To Kill a Mockingbird*

People should not worry so much about what they do but rather about what they are.

—Meister Eckhart

All groups and sectors of society desire to be taken seriously as citizens. Being heard and having an opportunity to influence and participate in the greater conversation or dialogue is indispensable. Voice, however, is not always about a collective group; individuals require it too. To have a voice, someone must listen.

Voice very simply is a desire to be acknowledged as an individual with standing, feelings, and thought. It goes beyond simply the sound of one's voice to actually being understood and accepted. Agreement is not the issue. Voice in this case means having one's perspectives acknowledged: being free to express oneself. Individuals feel safe and secure in their self-expression of concerns and ideas. Having a voice of one's own and a sense of freedom to use it does not rely on or require the approval of others. Voice comes with the spirit of independence and is self-revealing.

Voice comes from deep within—a person's inner self, their thoughts, hopes, dreams, viewpoint, philosophy. "Voice emerges literally from the body as a representation of our inner world. It carries our experience in the past, our hopes and fears for the future, and the emotional resonance of the moment. If it carries none of these, it must be a masked voice, and having muted the voice, anyone listening knows the person is not all there. Whether or not we try to tell the truth, the very act of speech is courageous because no matter what we say, we are revealed."[1] Desiring a voice takes resolution because trust is placed in the hands of another person to hear clearly and ethically: exposing the true self to the greater world takes mettle. Simple acknowledgment and appreciation as a human being are important to everyone.

Voice then, comes from a person's spirit and inner being. Words like heart, essence, emotion, and virtue relate to that concept and the inner voice within each person. It is important in problem-solving, self-concept, self-reflection, and critical thinking. A person's inner voice is the monologue of thoughts, which are usually tied to a person's sense of self.

The word courage concerns heart. Having a voice has to do with a heartfelt desire to discover what has meaning and passion in life. Pressure to pursue one's life can be thwarted without voice in their personal, social, or creative life. What drives people is often their passion, which is why they desire to have a voice that is heard and understood. Individuals who find their voice discover who they are and what they stand for, both requiring a sense of trust in oneself and one's perception of the world.

Passion does not always scream from the hilltop; sometimes, it arises within a person as a silent but potent force, intuitively and quietly, not with a flood of hyperkinetic energy, but expressed with great intensity and fervor. The individual becomes a participant in the larger community. Empowerment and deeper relationships open individuals to greater self-exposure and engagement in conversations about life and its challenges. With voice, people connect to the greater whole.

Listening to hear and understand a person's true voice requires being "fully conscious and aware in the present moment."[2] Distractions or personal detachment upset the ability to concentrate and listen. Being open beyond one's individual impressions and beliefs takes listening to a significant level.

Letting go of preconceptions allows the other person's voice to be heard. In a sense, it assists with knowing and understanding another person more deeply because experiencing their feelings and point of view takes place. Just being there and engaging in another person's world requires forsaking any readymade responses or solutions.

Empathic listening involves demonstrating care to others: that they are significant, though agreement is not always there. Being together person-to-person is at the core of helping people by truly listening to them, including their fears, feelings, and ambitions. Kindness involves opening one's heart and mind to others. Being sensitive to another's views and feelings helps them express themselves without fear. People are open and feel safe when others listen in this manner—it unlocks the doors to insight.

Communication in close relationships is indispensable. In marriages or other heartfelt engagements, empathy and affection create the intangible bonds that keep individuals together. Often in long relationships, a partner will say, "He truly understands me. She accepts me for who I am, along with my foibles, and doesn't try to remake me. Believe me, that is a true gift." In relationships that fragment and fall apart, the cause is commonly termed "poor communication," which frequently means that the person really doesn't "listen to me."

Silence is complex: it can be damaging or beneficial, and thoughtful or rejecting. Circumstances and emotions determine its impact: the content, relationship, history, and timing influence its tenor and intention and can communicate considerate agreement or severe discord and rejection.

In friendship, as well as other affectionate relationships, there is a need to express care and closeness. Giving and receiving these expressions are necessary for both people. The tall, silent prototype of "manly men" misses the mark here. In a loving relationship, both individuals need to feel secure to reveal feelings and to be acknowledged and accepted. Listening builds considerate and vital connections to both parties. Conversations about feelings and needs are not easy: they require a sense of care by really listening and taking the time and energy necessary to truly understand.

HUMBLE INQUIRY

Being empathetic and loving involves seeing life through another person's eyes. Everyone experiences life in their own way through their childhood experiences, relationships, education, philosophy, social network and other things that create their awareness and way of thinking. Significant events and relationships are life changing. Childhood experiences, in many cases, have a lifetime of impact, as do any experience that is heartfelt through achievement or loss.

Life brings lessons. Sometimes they emanate from discourse with others, and at other times, insight is gained from observing and feeling the emotion and passion of events. Wisdom is also shared by listening to the stories and interpretations of others: it does not always come from people with advanced degrees at prestigious universities or philosophers. The common person may have insight and astuteness because of their encounters and exposure to life and its hardships and toil. Perceptiveness and thoughtfulness are the byproducts not only of education but also of facing life with its warm and raw consequences.

Edgar Schein discusses humble inquiry, which is basically "the fine art of drawing someone out, of asking questions to which you do not already know the answer, of building a relationship based on curiosity and interest in the other person."[3] Three things are involved in this process.

First, doing less telling assists in developing a trusting relationship. American culture is built on telling, which often is interpreted as arrogance and self-importance. The implication being that the person does not know something that they should. Hence people feel compelled to interrupt and inform them why they were wrong. Humility is absent.

Second, doing more asking demonstrates an interest in the other person and a willingness to listen, which communicates a sense of humility to the speaker. Today's society emphasizes talking because it presents and demonstrates an image of capability and position, whereas the image of asking, to some, indicates subordination and lack of expertise. Wise individuals understand the value of good questions to gain insight

The obvious third component of humble inquiry is listening and acknowledging. Showing interest and listening not only to the subject matter of the message as indicated before but to its purpose and intention, which is critically important. Frequently people hear a phrase or sentence and assume that its intent is clear. Clarifying is a critically important aspect of listening and uncovers details and perspectives that are necessary for clarity.

Communication between two people can result in a meeting of the minds and hearts by which they openly share feelings, thoughts, desires, concerns, and understandings. Unpredictability exists in conversations. They can veer off into discussions that are touching and revealing or risky or deep. Sometimes the most impressive part of a conversation is the side roads people explore that lead to awareness and appreciation.

Conversations and listening bring people together as they gain insight into themselves, as well as the other person. These connections not only are cognitive but can also ignite emotional and spiritual bonds. Individuals, in a sense, become one—connected as a family, as a couple, as a friend, and as a colleague.

Learning blossoms from listening and conversing that generate rewarding relationships. Self and external discoveries come to light. Understanding of self and the greater society and life come from the personal interaction between the mind and the soul of others. Understanding self can come from the polestars in people's lives.

Polestars appear in people's lives and do not necessarily have any formal title. They are simply caring individuals with no incentive other than to help others reach the height of their talents and skills and to self-actualize. They provide honest feedback—both positive and difficult—in caring and thoughtful ways.

Polestars are mentors who make deep, substantial connections with people and provide awareness intellectually, morally, and emotionally. In a very caring way, they provide the individual with information about themselves that they need to know to be more effective and successful. They are passionate, lead through integrity, and stand on positive and caring values. They are people who touch the heart and spirit of another to help them live constructively and to meet their full potential and passion. They challenge individuals in both good and dark times. Their spirit excites minds and ignites the fire of motivation. Those personal conversations stand in the person receiving them as significant moments.

Polestars and leaders have several common attributes that cause individuals to connect with them. The primary one is a solid connection between the words and actions. They do not say one thing and do another. Their credibility of words and actions are tightly linked to values. The ends do not justify the means: ethics and principles matter.

Polestars set an example. They learn from mistakes and failures. Reaching important and desirable goals is a mission because without reaching them, meaning and satisfaction are lost. Polestars are frequently called upon to put events in proper perspective.

Polestars are authentic in their relationships because they are sincere and down to earth in words and actions. Ego driven behavior is absent. Active listening is an essential tool they apply in their relationships

These individuals understand the tangible and intangible forces at work. Relationships are founded on intangibles of understanding and passion and sincerity in courage. An open connection to people is primary, so that creativity and imagination can surface. Personal or organizational barriers are eliminated. The world is not always an orderly place because disequilibrium and chaos happen. Positive values and principles in relationships and organizations are necessary to self-organize and find the correct path.

Life is complex personally and socially and is filled with ideas, feelings, and ambitions, as well as a potpourri of relationships. All human beings, regardless of gender, race, ethnicity, or any other factors, have the same emotional, physical, and intellectual needs. They desire connection to friends, family, colleagues, or others. Communication is a pathway for the recognition, affection, and relationships they need.

A difference exists between friends and contacts. Human presence and energy are extremely powerful: a hug has tangible and intangible elements that cannot be replicated by any technology or artificial intelligence. Human beings need emotional warmth, understanding, and consideration of others. Computer codes cannot replicate feelings and emotions—an emotional teardrop cannot be programmed. No surefire recipe exists for creating close relationships. Powerful intangibles exist that create emotional ties and mutual compassion.

A true friend is created through care, acceptance, and understanding, which takes time and trust. Friendships generally have a history and, in many, common interests and similar values. In difficult and trying times, friends offer an emotional bond that moves beyond a click on a keyboard. Cultivating friendships and other relationships requires being fully present and engaging personally with others. Research shows that individuals long to identify with people in a compassionate and authentic way. Relationships are essential for happiness in life.

A study by BlueCross BlueShield on the health of Americans, entitled *Major Depression: Impact on Overall Health*, found that "diagnosis of major depression has risen dramatically by 33% since 2013."[4] Millennial's depression rate increased 47 percent, and adolescent boys and girls by 47 percent and 65 percent, respectively.

PEW research cites the same trend, finding increases in anxiety and depression by teens across income boundaries amounting to 70 percent, 73 percent, and 67 percent, with families of incomes of <30,000, 30,000–74,999, and 75,000+, respectively. The increases were seriously high for all financial categories. Obviously, economic circumstances alone are not the cause.

Pressures emanate from social acceptance, school relationships, future expectations, and bullying. Whether teens or adults, depression and its causes create health and social issues. People need to be acknowledged socially and emotionally. Feeling connected and accepted by others is a major factor.

Today, there is virtual reality, which is not reality at all. Technology distracts people from their failures or anxiety. Some check into virtual reality, escaping life and withdrawing into a technological artificial experience. Individuals miss the opportunity to encounter real situations with real people—technological escape will not solve the need for relationships, but can actually exacerbate it.

Software cannot create human sensitivity or concern—it can only come from within the individual or group. "Without experiencing that others know us, or are able to, we're left feeling alone—at times, disparagingly so. It's a bleak place to be and can lead to feelings of emptiness and despondency."[5] Individuals desire attachment to something larger than themselves.

Feeling connected socially is satisfying and nurturing and helps develop relationships with others even though, as individuals, they may not be close friends. Finding one's passion acts as a connector socially and individually because common interests open doors to others and deepen relationships.

Times exist where individuals seek the ability to contemplate life, nature, and self because it can be hectic and busy, without the quiet necessary for self-reflection and feeling. It is a personal, not imposed, decision to stop and find respite in one's thoughts and emotions.

Solitude is not synonymous with loneliness; it actually allows people to be introspective and to seek understanding of their own true self. Solitude is restorative in a busy and, at times, disorderly world. Loneliness differs from solitude, which is a personal decision—a unilateral one that the person makes, not the feeling of exclusion perpetrated by the decisions of others. Individuals can sit in solitude and feel fulfilled: being an observer locked out of social relationships is not.

Ironically, one can feel loneliness when within a group of people. A sense of social isolation exists because the values and principles of the group collide with those of the individual. Others may see a person as connected, but loneliness is a subjective experience—it is real and exists in the mind of the person. Shyness and insecurity, however, can lead to a lack of social contact. Personal relationships take time to develop, and not interacting with others because of shyness or insecurity can be misinterpreted as a lack of interest or arrogance.

Loneliness, unlike solitude, is different and comes from other circumstances and conditions. For some individuals, safety resides in silence, not expressing one's true self, and not risking voice. Isolation, abandonment, and friendlessness are feelings of individuals who are lonely. A lack of connection—something or somebody is missing—carries a mental burden, which is unlike the solitude of sitting with nature and contemplating life.

As poet David Whyte expressed, "Loneliness is the doorway to unspecified desire. In the bodily pain of aloneness is a first step to understanding how far we are from a real friendship, from a proper work or a long-sought love. Loneliness can be a prison, a place from a which we look out at a world we cannot inhabit; loneliness can be a bodily ache and a penance, but loneliness fully inhabited also becomes the voice that asks and calls for that great, unknown someone or something else we want to call our own."[6]

Abraham Maslow's need hierarchy clearly defines people's needs for belongingness and love through friends and more intimate relationships. Interpersonal connections are at the core of belonging and acceptance. Maslow's Hierarchy of Needs[7] concerns the backdrop for why having a voice is important. All people have fundamental issues concerning the need for affection and self-esteem. In Maslow's model, people require basic needs to be met that include physiological (food, shelter, etc.) and safety (personal security, health, etc.). Once these are fulfilled, individuals have higher order needs to include "love, affection, and belongingness."

Most people have a desire to be accepted: to be able to be genuinely oneself that results in openness and trust with another. Not everyone feels secure or trusting to be open to others. When openness begins to evaporate, conversation and sharing are restricted.

In a large sense, total rejection or acceptance of others can lead to indifference—a loss of interest, feeling, or reaction to someone. Indifference is an extremely powerful force in dehumanizing people and negating their value and presence.

History is replete with indifference in many times and cultures. Elie Wiesel, in a speech entitled, *The Perils of Indifference*, stated:

What is indifference? Etymologically, the word means "no difference." A strange and unnatural state in which the lines blur between light and darkness, dusk and dawn, crime and punishment, cruelty and compassion, good and evil. . . . Of course, indifference can be tempting—more than that, seductive. It is so much easier to look away from victims. It is so much easier to avoid such rude interruptions to our work, our dreams, our hopes. It is, after all, awkward, troublesome, to be involved in another person's pain and despair. Yet, for the person who is indifferent, his or her neighbor are of no consequence. And, therefore, their lives are meaningless. Their hidden or even visible anguish is of no interest. Indifference reduces the other to an abstraction."[8]

Individuals confronting indifference face extreme measures and attitudes geared to silencing their voices so they cannot be heard, understood, or recognized. During the Holocaust, Nazi policies silenced ethical and moral standards and incited indifference toward aggressive tactics. Indifference is dismissive and callous of an individual's humanity, welfare, or fate. With indifference, the people's voice is silent, and lives are dishonored.

NOTES

1. David Whyte, *The Heart Aroused* (New York: Currency Doubleday, 1994), 120.

2. Peter M. Senge, et al., *Presence: An Exploration of Profound Change in People, Organizations, and Society* (The Crown Publishing Group, 2005), Loc 230, Kindle.

3. Edgar H. Schein, *Humble Inquiry: The Gentle Art of Asking Instead of Telling* (Barrett-Koehler Publishers, 2013), 2–11, Kindle.

4. Blue Cross Blue Shield, *Major Depression: Impact on Overall Health*, May 10, 2018, https://www.bcbs.com/the-health-of-america/reports/major-depression-the-impact-overall-health.

5. Leon F. Seltzer, "Feeling Understood—Even More Important Than Feeling Loved," *Psychology Today*, June 28, 2017.

6. David Whyte, *Consolations: The Solace, Nourishment and Underlying Meaning of Everyday Words* (Langley, Washington: Many Rivers Press, 2015), 131.

7. Abraham H. Maslow, *A Theory of Human Motivation* (Psychology Classics, 1943), Loc 1156–1198, www.all-about-psychology.com.

8. Elie Wiesel, *The Perils of Indifference*, https://americanrhetoric.com/speeches/ewieselperilsofindifference.html.

Chapter 6

Active Listening

You cannot truly listen to anyone and do anything else at the same time.

—M. Scott Peck

Never miss a good chance to shut up.

—Will Rogers

Active listening seems like an oxymoronic term. Yes, listeners must be quiet and fully reflective of what the person is saying. Being quiet is necessary, but on the other hand, it must be cognitively active. Listening is not a passive or indifferent activity—it requires attention and commitment. The question is: what is active listening?

Sandra Day O'Connor, former Supreme Court Justice, was an effective leader on the court. One of her main assets was skillful listening, which became evident to O'Connor's law clerks and others who noticed her body language. "She took time to listen, and as she listened, she would become almost unnaturally still. Her bright, penetrating hazel eyes would focus intently. She conveyed that her whole being was paying attention, because it was."[1]

According to aides, she knew when and how to listen, allowing her to have a greater impact on her colleagues and the decisions of the court. She built bridges and did not engage in raging or arrogant monologues. In addition, she had a sense of humor. O'Connor's example highlights the importance of sincere listening, whether on issues of law, at work, or in one-on-one conversations with colleagues, family, or friends. Listening is a critical skill and a major foundation for quality relationships of all kinds.

In the "The Lost Art of Listening," Jim McNamara stated that there are several tenets for effective listening.[2] The first is recognition of the right of individuals or groups to speak. No one should be marginalized or limited in their ability to be heard. With today's technology, categorizing, name-calling, and labeling people obstructs discussion and ultimately leads to a breakdown of democratic standards and debate.

Second, individuals should be recognized and acknowledged as they express themselves verbally, in letters, or through e-mails and technology. Attention to others and interpreting and understanding what is stated accurately and fairly is vital, even in moments of emotion or conflict. Genuine consideration of what individuals said and why they said it is essential.

Closing one's mind to the perspective of others is a detriment to fully comprehend the message and to the ability to agree or even agree to disagree. In essence, closed or apathetic minds marginalize them, particularly if individuals do not understand their own prejudices or mindsets.

What really matters is being listened to respectfully, because it demonstrates regard for the person, not the agreement, with the individual's stance. Many people enjoy a conversation where a friendly debate provides opportunities to learn and consider one's own thinking. Listening allows people to safely be together and to be cognizant of each other's thoughts and being.

The ideas and propositions of others require strength of character because the listeners must push some of their own views into the background and focus. The risk is that what they hear may require a reassessment of their own views. New or challenging ideas can be persuasive and bring about reform. In conversation, listeners may review their own thinking and be open to adopting a different or modified perspective.

To do so, several prerequisites are necessary. Obviously, openness is fundamental in the process of listening, which begins with "wanting to know" and being free from bias or prejudgments of another person, philosophies, or ideas. This is a minimal requirement.

Removing stereotypes and other barriers in communication is a prerequisite. Considering views and opinions and understanding differences is necessary. Discerning the "what" of a person's communication also requires recognizing the "why" they feel as they do. Sometimes it's experience, education, or any number of things that set their perspective. Determining what people think and why they feel as they do is an important foundation for understanding.

Listening and thinking about ideas, as well as the underlying rationale, require time. Significant attention is necessary to fairly assimilate and interpret the other person's ideas fairly and to acknowledge their perspective.

Accordingly, listening involves a number of processes.[3] First, a process to receive, comprehend, and interpret content is required. Second, understanding the person's affect—their feelings and desires—necessitates listening actively and empathically. Finally, a behavioral aspect of listening includes responding with feedback verbally and nonverbally, for example, paraphrasing, asking questions, eye contact, nodding, and others. While listeners need to be verbally quiet to fully understand, they must be active in terms of being mindful.

"Active listening can be used to hear accurately, understand, draw out ideas and information, empathize, gather information, show respect, build self-esteem, find answers, show appreciation, buy time, connect, question assumptions and ideas, weigh options, change perspective, soothe or heal, set the stage for something else, and build relationships."[4]

The point is that active listening can be applied in a multitude of fields and for a variety of purposes. As a listening tool that can be applied in formal and informal, professional and routine, and individual or group circumstances, active listening can generate clearer and deeper connections.

Two things are very important with active listening. One is to interpret the substance of messages—the communication itself: what the words and sentences mean. Second, comprehending the purpose of the communication. "In active listing you clarify the content and intent of messages in a nonjudgmental manner. Simply saying 'I hear you say that you are frustrated with . . .' or 'I sense that you are angry about . . .' and listening to the response can make a big difference in promoting understanding and letting the person know you are interested and comprehend his or her full meaning."[5]

A key goal is exploring each other's reasoning and fully recognizing what they think and why. Active listening requires mental energy and presumes that the other person has something to offer. Certainly, silence is essential, but so are thinking, asking pertinent questions, and clarifying statements.

Tools that can be helpful in this process include paraphrasing, clarifying, reflecting, and summarizing. Roadblocks include judging, threatening, diagnosing, minimizing, and other attempts to fix, evaluate, divert, or interrupt the speaker and process.

Active listening's primary focus is building relationships and trust through respectful rapport and creating a foundation for working together to examine issues and options. Through this, people feel free to talk because someone is really listening without judgment. With this connection, tension and defensiveness are reduced, and any conflicts have a greater opportunity to be identified and resolved because information and feelings are conveyed and acknowledged.

Issues cannot be settled if they are not clearly defined or discerned from a variety of viewpoints. Listening actively increases the prospect of hearing accurately because ideas and information are clarified, and perception, problems, and possible solutions are defined. It is not a technological regimen or investigation—it has a human element to it that is critical.

Showing empathy and respecting the other person results in a sensitive relationship and the opportunity to develop constructive associations and possibly something more. Acceptance of others, not necessarily agreement, builds the possibility of more interaction and dialogue.

Human relationships are the result of compassion—being able to talk and be considerate with each other creates a bond and a mutual and open communication highway. Today's impersonal text and email vehicles exist far from the ability to listen actively: they are about talking or, in many cases, spouting a position and derogatorily painting others in a negative light. Many quips and retorts are condescending. Depth in relationships comes from patience and acceptance of why people feel as they do. Being physically together reveals subtle and obvious emotion and passion that technological messages cannot.

True listening and communication require undivided attention, eye contact, and mental focus. The person talking must perceive that the other individual is engaged in genuine and sincere listening. Feedback in the form of clarification of assumptions and expressions is an important aspect of this process. Listeners must express verbally or nonverbally understanding of the sentiments and content of the conversation.

As part of dialogue, appreciating the personal or professional influence of one's comments or actions on others is helpful. Learning the other person's story and perspective is beneficial in finding areas of priority and mutual attachment. On the other side of the ledger, expressing individual thoughts and feelings helps others recognize another's perspective. In each case, clarity, honesty, and respect must be apparent—and they must go both ways.

When people understand each other, they are able to address challenges and circumstances together. Each person learns something about the other, which is critical and necessary in order to develop a respectful context for conversation and moving forward. Finding a common purpose based on mutual respect is at the core of understanding.

Carl Rogers and Richard Farson stated that "we have learned to think of ourselves in certain, definitive ways. We have built up pictures of ourselves. Sometimes, these self-pictures are pretty realistic but at other times they are not."[6] In conversations, both speakers and listeners may feel they have to defend themselves and their self-images. Or their self-image may cause them not to engage because of the reputation or stature of the other person.

These circumstances can be threatening, and the discussion deteriorates into a defensive mode eliminating any introspective insight that can come from it. Any presenter must be aware that the viewpoint of others may differ from their own, but it does not mean they are antagonistic or disrespectful. Defensiveness creates problems. Differing views do not have to be hostile. Arrogance is expecting others to always agree with one's position or not being introspective enough to self-reflect on the viability of different ideas or opinions.

Hence, that's why active listening is different from a tit-for-tat exchange of comments and comebacks. Listeners, at times, feel they must have answers and provide advice to the other person and solve issues. The speaker may not need or desire an outside opinion or guidance. In fact, they may be thinking through the issues themselves in the conversation. They may just need someone to listen to their story and be heard.

On the other hand, however, listeners are placed in a circumstance where the speaker wants or sometimes demands opinions or evaluations. This also can stifle open and honest conversation because the listener may not be comfortable in that role or have the necessary expertise or wisdom. They may feel uneasy offering a position or recommendation because they do not have the insight or do not feel the responsibility to provide information or recommendations. Expecting judgments to be made immediately limits open and honest conversation. The matter in question my require more time, data, or investigation because significant judgments necessitate time, investigation, and reflection.

Openness is a main pillar—the attention and receptivity to people, and the work at hand. Interpretation involves defining and creating meaning, the foundation of which is knowledge and making sense of what is heard.

Several precautions are important in active listening. Frequently when people listen, they slip into trying to change the speaker's perspective on things and want them to adopt the approach of the listener through prodding, encouraging, reasoning, or other methods. In most of these cases, listeners respond to their needs, not those of the speaker. It is difficult for both listeners and speakers to accept decisions or actions that differ from their own.

A corollary problem is the continuous urging of the speaker for listeners to respond to issues and assessments. "Do you agree or disagree?" Constant calls for agreement or disagreement, which concern the need for endorsement of their feelings and needs, as well as their solutions to issues. This can actually create an unnecessary distraction for the listener.

A problem exists in passing judgment whether it is requested or offered, because it restricts free expression: speakers may feel that there is an effort to correct, not understand, them. Trying to encourage a speaker to adopt a particular position is often perceived as an effort to transform them or have them recognize their errors. This can be viewed as useless and stops conversation.

On the other hand, pure optimism is not always helpful either—it can be perceived as a means to stop listening and engaging. When in the course of serious conversation, such phrases from the listener, even encouragingly—"I am sure everything will work out for you," or "sounds good to me!"—are not helpful. It basically is perceived that the person is tired of listening and wants to move on.

Effective active listening includes several key behaviors:[7]

- Seeing and grasping the speaker's point of view: what is really being communicated. Getting inside the person's perspective is essential.
- Listening for total meaning, both the content of the message and the philosophy or perspective underlying it.
- Feelings are important and a part of all communication. At times, they are at the core of the message and must be recognized. Being sensitive to both substance and objective is a necessity.
- Sensitivity to cues is necessary in defining meaning. Cues are not always verbal, and often come through expression, tone and level of voice, and hesitations, and inflections. To understand requires more than simply hearing and interpreting words and concepts correctly.

Active listening demonstrates a true interest in the speaker and his or her message. Time is necessary in listening, and that commitment demonstrates that the person is committed and respectfully there and is attentive. It demonstrates caring to really understand a person and their perspective without the goal of changing them or "setting them straight." Presence and respect are demonstrated, not simply stated.

When people really listen actively, others gain clarity on issues, their needs, and possible outcomes. Telling and debating are frequently perceived to be the only ways and means to engage in conversation personally or professionally. However, through active listening, constructive behaviors are learned and true connections are made and validated.

Perceiving and comprehending the world as others see it develop trust and receptiveness that open doors to problem-solving, and self-renewal of both parties. Active listening is more than hearing: it includes emotional consideration, appreciation, and respect for the life and emotions of others.

NOTES

1. Evan Thomas, "Sandra Day O'Connor's Lessons in Leadership," *Wall Street Journal*, March 7, 2019.

2. Jim McNamara, "The Lost Art of Listening," *Public Lecture, London School of Economics*, November 23, 2016, http://www.lse.ac.uk/assets/richmedia/channels/publicLecturesAndEvents/transcripts/20161123_1830_theLostArtOfListening_tr.pdf.

3. Graham D. Brodie, "Issues in the Measurement of Listening," *Communication Research Reports*, Vol. 30, No. 1, January–March 2013, 17.

4. Joseph Topornycky and Shaya Golparian, "Building Openness and Interpretation in Active Listening," *Collective Essays on Learning and Teaching (CELT)*, Vol. IX, 2016, 176.

5. George A. Goens, *Soft Leadership for Hard Times* (Lanham, MD: Rowman & Littlefield, 2005), 89–90.

6. Carl R. Rogers and Richard E. Farson, *Active Listening* (Mansfield Centre, CT: Martino Publishing, 2015), 5.

7. Rogers and Farson, *Active Listening*.

Chapter 7

Dialogue

Now if we think together, then maybe we can solve our common problems.

—David Bohm

Communication is generally thought of as conversation. However, conversation is not singular in form: there are several types with different expectations, goals, interactions, and outcomes. Most everyone has experienced them: speeches, debates, orders, monologues, dialogues, and others. They all have a specific purpose and outcome.

However, some criticism or tirades, in particular, are not easy to experience because of their one-sided velocity. Generally, they are also called monologues or rants, with individuals pontificating positively or negatively, angrily, or passionately about issues and situations. Diatribes are simply one-way harangues that are emotional, and passionate, about issues, policies, behavior, values, or any other number of questions or concerns. Everyone, at one time or another, has heard them—"Let me tell you a thing or two about . . ." or "You're wrong! You don't know what you're talking about." Emotion is the foundation for them, but in some cases, they occur because people do not feel heard and are frustrated or angry.

Another form of discourse is debate, which is engaging others in a two-way contest marked by the competitive goal to simply convince others of one's viewpoint or solution. Another person or persons are involved in listening, and comments go back-and-forth between each. It is simply comment and retort—a counter to the other person's remarks. Finding agreement or solutions is not always the objective: winning the debate is!

Diatribe and debate are both highly aggressive and insistent. Expressing emotions and convincing others is the sole purpose. At times direct confrontation may be necessary; for example, confronting the moral and ethical implications of actions or behavior.

At times, it is necessary to give orders. Emergencies or crises require direct orders. They are vital because there is no time for debate or discussion: individuals must cooperate to get things done. Timing is of the essence of people having to respond directly and safely. One-way directions and instructions in certain situations are a necessity to remedy the circumstances. Quite simply, orders are efficient and accepted in times of emergency. Parents, public officials, military officers, police, firefighters, and anyone facing difficult or disastrous circumstances will call out orders.

In other situations, persuasion is necessary. Business leaders, politicians, parents, and other professional advisers persuade individuals to take the "right" course. To do so, credibility must exist because if the communicator is not trusted, communication falls on deaf ears. Without trust, passion will be perceived as insincere, and reason will be considered as biased and self-promotional. From trust comes genuineness and respect, and with those, listening is possible.

Mortimer Adler stated, "Reasons and arguments may be used to reinforce the drive of the passions, but reasons and arguments will have no force at all unless your listeners are already disposed emotionally to move in the direction that your reasons and arguments tried to justify."[1] More than words are necessary to be convincing. Strong emotional allegiance can supersede logic.

Today's society, however, requires deeper levels of discussion and listening beyond ego and winning. One opinion in convoluted situations is not sufficient to find real approaches and effective decisions. Complex problems require thinking anew in order to find successful paths rather than simply peddling sales pitches. Diatribes, debates and verbal counterpunching will not bring about understanding or commitment: they divide and push people rather than encourage true exchange of ideas. Verbal ping-pong results and people do not come together because they are not heard or refuse to engage.

> Discussion is almost like a ping-pong game, where people are batting the ideas back and forth and the object of the game is to win or to get points for yourself. Possibly you will take up somebody else's ideas to back up your own—you may agree with some and disagree with others—but the basic point is to win the game.[2]

DIALOGUE—THE WHAT

Dialogue is different from the other forms of communication. It is not about winning. It is not about convincing. It is not about following orders. It is not about ego. It is much deeper.

David Bohm stated,

> In a dialogue . . . nobody is trying to win. Everybody wins if anybody wins. There is a different sort of spirit to it. In a dialogue, there is no attempt to gain points, or to make your particular view prevail. Rather, whenever any mistake is discovered on the part of anybody, everybody gains. It's a situation called win-win, whereas the other game is win-lose—if I win, you lose. But a dialogue is something more of a common participation, in which we are not playing a game against each other, but with each other. In a dialogue, everybody wins.[3]

Dialogue is from *dialogos*, a Greek word. Logos means "the word" and dia means "through" [not two because a dialogue can be a number of people]. Individuals can even have a dialogue with themselves. A dialogue is much more than a discussion as Bohm stated: "Contrast this with the word 'discussion,' which has the same root as 'percussion' and 'concussion.' It really means to break things up. It emphasizes the idea of analysis, where there may be many points of view, and where everybody is presenting a different one—analyzing and breaking up."[4]

William Isaacs defined dialogue as "shared inquiry, a way of thinking and reflecting together. It is not something you do to a person. It is something you do with another person."[5] The intent of dialogue is not to take sides, but to reach a new understanding—discovering a new foundation from which to think and act. Collective intelligence is important, particularly because insight from a number of sources can be invaluable in broadening perspectives and ideas. Diversity of thought is extremely important in these circumstances.

Isaacs believes dialogue is a conversation—not with sides, but with a center. Individuals are equals in dialogue: they all have the same status and responsibility. Examining differences to come to a new understanding and formulate the ability to think anew is the goal. Connecting together to listen deeply to each other and examining the possibility of something new unfolding is the result.

WHY DIALOGUE?

Communication should enhance learning and help people get out of their intellectual and emotional shells. Life presents immediate challenges and problems, as well as those on the horizon. All call for much more than talking or pontificating because changes in all facets of society require new perceptions and perspectives. "Tried-and-true" ideas and strategies may no longer be pertinent as society and relationships evolve.

What dialogue can do, contrary to some other forms of communication, is to create new possibilities and ways to think about things. Individuals and organizations have mental models that drive their interpretation, thinking, and decisions. In organizations and society, established patterns of shared assumptions and expectations exist that direct thought and direction. The problem is that they may be out of tune with the times or the evolutions that have taken place.

Transformations historically have altered society creating new patterns of thought and possibilities, as well as unforeseen questions and problems. In the past, Newtonian science viewed the world mechanistically, while today chaos theory and self-organizing systems take a different view.

Newton helped shape the rational view of the world that, in essence, operates on simple principles like a machine. There is an aura of predictability based on established rules. Newtonian logic is based on taking any complex phenomenon and reducing it to its individual components: its smallest possible parts. Then, the interaction of the parts can be analyzed to determine their regular and expected behavior.

Hierarchical structures and separate roles and command structures slice and dice individuals and processes into specific parts and roles. This results in fragmented thought. Shared meaning between all individuals is lost in this Newtonian view of organizations.

Chaos theory, however, explains the unpredictability of the nonlinear side of the universe. While Newtonian science explains gravity and electrical reactions, Chaos theory concerns the unpredictability of issues like weather, turbulence, people's brain states, and the stock market. Understanding that the world has chaotic and complex systems provides a different interpretation than simple routine cause-and-effect of Newtonian logic. One example is the "Butterfly Effect," which involves small changes causing dramatic and transformational shifts, for example, a butterfly fluttering wings in China creates a hurricane in Iowa.

Historically, the "Butterfly Effect" has been at work. For example, the use of a piece of masking tape, it could be argued, led to the impeachment of a president. A Watergate building security guard discovered a basement door with two locks had been taped open with masking tape. At first, he thought employees placed the tape there for the ease of entry and not having to use a key to enter. He removed the tape and went about his rounds. When he returned later, the guard discovered the door had been re-taped. He became suspicious of a robbery, and he called authorities. Two police officers responded in an unmarked police car without sirens. They entered the build-ing and arrested the perpetrators. As a result, the historic Watergate scandal unfolded, resulting in the demise of a president.

> The new sciences of chaos theory, self-organizing systems, and quantum phys-ics tell us about the value of dialogue in the modern world. They point out how both the roots of, as well as the solution to, our current dilemmas spring from the very worldviews we hold. Images and ways of working based on seventeenth-century physics are now limiting us as we try to meet twenty-first-century challenges. The old, or Newtonian, views of how to organize and manage organizations are not only insufficient for facing our core dilemmas, but are, in certain cases, the cause of them.[6]

Changes can present problems and conflicts. Silence, then, is not a virtue. Perceiving all problems through the same lens of the past can result in miss-ing and not addressing real circumstances. When people feel they cannot contribute, their silence can be very damaging. Ideas are suppressed and per-spective curtailed causing a loss of creativity and reasoning. Not participat-ing and withholding information is done in order to maintain the established norms and relationships.

Thinking about the world and society through the contemporary-scientific lens presents different perspectives on issues and solutions rather than exam-ining it from a mechanistic view. While there are solid principles governing the universe, it is not always a machine with lockstep operations. Butterfly wings have impact. Chaos exists. Dialogue can bring about a new way of thinking as things emerge from the unexpected power of collective thought and insight. Concepts or establish processes may fall out of line with contem-porary issues and times.

Dialogue emphasizes thinking, reviewing, and challenging the assumptions under which things operate. Consciously examining how the thought process works, the group can think better collectively, as well as communicate more effectively. Listening actively is an essential part of dialogue as individuals participate and ideas are expressed. Actually, dialogue is a means to think together by suspending judgment and certainty. Listening is very important in this process, as individuals explain their outlook and analyses. Listening openly without resistance or judgment is imperative, along with respecting the integrity of another's viewpoint. Too often, people cannot let go of their own judgments and believe what they think is without question. At times, people are trying to solve the wrong problem: they miss what the real issue is.

Dialogue focuses on creative problem identification as well as problem-solving. The focus is not on direct and personal encounters. In dialogue, "The whole group is the object of learning, and members share the potential excitement of discovery, collectively, ideas that individually none of them might have ever thought."[7] The focus is on dialogue and feedback, which occurs only if their direct behavior supports the natural flow of the dialogue. Roles and positions are not the mainspring for reflection. Everyone has equal participation in the dialogue.

Dialogue opens three doors: the good, the true, and the beautiful.[8] The good concerns ethics and collective action, the true is the pursuit of objective scientific truth, and the beautiful focuses on aesthetics and art. Hopefully, dialogue enables participants to overcome fragmentation through this common inquiry. Working together in unison develops energy that binds individuals together and raises the opportunity to create with others the possibility of solving problems or, at least, defining issues that must be addressed so success is possible.

Individuals and organizations want to find meaning and success, and participation is more than simply receiving recognition and fiscal compensation. It is beautiful when people's minds and spirit come together in common purpose. The intrinsic issues that cause people to participate lead to greater commitment and possibilities.

Finding meaning and value are intrinsic motivators, and dialogue properly implemented speaks to these intrinsic motivators.[9] Engaging in dialogue involves four pillars.

- Purpose: significance, meaning, impact, and service
- Principles: integrity, ethics, morality, goodness, truth, and dignity
- People: belonging, connection, community, recognition, and respect
- Autonomy: creativity, achievement, learning, and self-mastery

Dialogue brings people together to examine thinking, challenges, mindsets, opportunities, approaches, perspectives, and collaboration. The goal is not to maintain control but to digest the issues and points of view and collectively determine the best course. In doing so, the process operates in principle and not in power or ego, and it provides individuals with the opportunity to participate in a creative learning experience.

Dialogue entails listening, thinking, and creating meaning with others. Participation in dialogue involves shared meaning developed through deliberating and reflecting together. The development of shared meaning and common understanding results in people working together and pursuing actions important to improvement and success. It is not about competition; it concerns thinking collectively from all possibilities. Creating an inclusive environment for dialogue to take place is imperative because there are blocks that can handicap it from taking place. There must be an appropriate culture for collaboration for successful dialogue.

Collective thinking results in clear awareness and understanding of circumstances that leads to transformation. In dialogue, it is important for people to realize what is on each other's minds without coming to any conclusion or judgment. Judgments are evaluations that draw simple comparisons of good-bad, intelligence-dense, or yes-no. Suspending judgment is a positive measure enabling the individual and others the opportunity to reflect and consider possibilities and move beyond stereotypes that frequently end discussions.

In argumentative and polarized situations, stagnation develops: people don't respond or share. People stop thinking about maintaining a fallacious harmony. They operate based on past behavior and ideas, along with memory, which, in reality, does not involve much thinking.

Fragmentation is a serious issue because individuals defend their perceptions or ideas based on their mindset, even in the face of evidence to the contrary. That is why in dialogue, reviewing mindsets, thinking, and assumptions are necessary. Thought is basic—it produces understanding and options. New ways of thinking open the doors to new ways of perceiving and solving issues.

Dialogue builds relationships as individuals discuss how they perceive and think about the organization or challenges. Relationships, respect, and trust are essential for people to participate and listen. Openness to perspectives and approaches to analyze thinking produce a context to focus on what is unfolding, what is evident, and the issues they bring.

Participants must listen to themselves: understanding their biases, perceptions, and filters in their own thinking. Without that, they become blind to their own preferences and weaknesses as listeners. Then individuals can really listen.

DIALOGUE—HOW

To have a true dialogue, several things are required so that each individual can contribute. First, no one has to feel competitive pressure to gain standing. Dialogue is successful when everyone feels they are all in it together. Dialogue is not negotiation. People don't have to be defensive—assumptions may differ, but those differences may spur new thought, insight, and approaches.

In dialogue sessions, everyone should feel as equal as possible. Rank does not matter. Titles and position status should not be highlighted: everyone is coequal sitting in a circle. This leads to ensuring that everyone has a voice and encourages and ensures that everyone can comment. This may take some time and patience as participants realize and understand how it works. Everyone's participation is encouraged and legitimized.

In American, society action is a primary principle. "Let's act and get something done." In emergencies or severe crises, this may be necessary, as indicated earlier. Sometimes, individuals perceive thinking as not action and not getting anything accomplished. They are impatient, want to jump into taking action, and thrust themselves in the role of telling others what needs to get done in order to move on. Arrogance is dysfunctional, and collective thought is powerful.

In actuality, the process of dialogue can lead to self-revision of one's thinking and viewpoint if the penchant to defend one's opinions and assumptions is suspended. Bohm emphasized, "In the dialogue group we are not going to decide what to do about anything. This is crucial. Otherwise we are not free. We must have an empty space where we are not obliged to do anything, nor to come to any conclusions, nor to say anything or not say anything. It's open and free. It's an empty space. . . . Our purpose is really to communicate coherently in truth, if you want to call that a purpose."[10]

The purpose of dialogue is a means of deliberation in order to build common understanding. As part of this process, an individual should see the "hidden meanings" of their own communication.

Action, however, has to be based on critical thought and complete understanding. That is why suspending assumptions and judgments are necessary in a dialogue. Before concrete decisions are made, exploring perspectives and determining truth in light of what is transforming and changing is necessary. Suspending judgments—not suppressing or immediately acting on them— also eliminates the penchant to debate or negotiate.

Schein proposed,

Dialogue, on the other hand, is a basic process for building common understanding, in that it allows one to see the hidden meanings of words, first by seeing such hidden meanings in our own communication. By letting disagreement go, meanings become clearer, and the group gradually builds a shared set of meanings that make much higher levels of mutual understanding and creative thinking possible. As we listen to others and ourselves in what may appear often to be a disjointed, rather random conversation, we begin to see the bias and subtleties of how each member thinks and expresses meanings. In this process, we do not convince each other, but build a common experience base that allows us to learn collectively. The more the group has achieved such collective understanding, the easier it becomes to reach decisions, and the more likely it will be that the decision will be implemented in the way that the group meant it.[11]

By developing a sense of shared meaning, the group can coalesce, and individuals can discuss issues in a nonjudgmental context. Listening is a primary skill in creating this sense. Shared meaning holds a group together.

Relationships are key in any social or work environment. Being interconnected means moving away from separate parts, roles, perspectives, and responsibilities to a deeper connection that is fixed on the whole—"we're in this together." Seeing the whole picture is necessary to understand the total impact.

Confronting and understanding one's own personal assumptions and those of others, along with the feelings behind them, can lead to building common ground. From this point as a group, shared assumptions can be identified, and a common understanding can be constructed. Collaboration can occur to find solutions and resolution to issues, problems, or conflicts.

Ellinor and Gerard summarized what the practice of dialogue could do. "As dialogue is practiced over time, we discover (1) greater levels of authenticity showing up, (2) better decisions being made, and (3) improved morale and alignment forming around shared work. More personal initiative and leadership are exercised outside of the formal hierarchy. As people begin to see more of the whole of what is being accomplished together, they each see where he/she can add more value. People stop waiting for someone else to tell them what to do."[12]

NOTES

1. Mortimer J. Adler, *How to Speak How to Listen* (Touchstone, 1997), 37, Kindle.

2. David Bohm, *On Dialogue* (Taylor and Francis, 2012), 7, Kindle.

3. Bohm, *On Dialogue*, 7.

4. Bohm, *On Dialogue*, 7.

5. William Isaacs, *Dialogue and the Art of Thinking Together* (New York: Currency Publishers, 1999), 9.

6. Linda Ellinor and Glenna Gerard, *Dialogue: Rediscover the Transforming Power of Conversatio* (Crossroad Press, 2014), Loc 1075, Kindle.

7. Edgar H. Schein, "Dialogue, Culture, and Organizational Learning," *Reflections*, Vol. 4, No. 4.

8. Isaacs, *Dialogue and the Art of Thinking Together*, 13.

9. Fred Kofman, *The Meaning Revolution: The Power of Transcendent Leadership* (The Crown Publishing Group, 2018), 121, Kindle.

10. Kofman, *The Meaning Revolution*, 19.

11. Schein, "Dialogue, Culture, and Organizational Learning," 34.

12. Ellinor and Gerard, *Dialogue*, Loc 1091.

Chapter 8

Mindsets

It is the mark of an educated mind to be able to entertain a thought without accepting it.

—Aristotle

We must have strong minds, ready to accept facts as they are.

—Harry S. Truman

"Just sit and listen!" Sounds easy, but is it? The assumption is that if someone sits quietly, they are listening—they are tuned in. While the body is steady and silent, much more is going on affecting whether or not the person is really attentive. What is happening is invisible to the eye. The mind is at work.

Feelings, thoughts, reactions, and more circle the mind of the prospective listener. They pop up even though the intention is to listen. A statement or an internal thought can spark all kinds of feelings: anger, frustration, joy, or doubt, or a variety of others. In addition, beliefs and experiences raise assumptions and prejudices.

Emotions can skew communication and lead to an inaccurate analysis. Feelings influence thoughts and thoughts affect feelings. In a way, the relationship between both is reflexive based on past events and impressions. Individuals develop a philosophy and understanding based on their encounters and education, which trigger both emotional and cognitive reactions and impulses. Perception is a significant filter in listening and other forms of communication. Beliefs strongly sway assessments of reality.

THE MIND AND LISTENING

Everyone has a way of thinking and people do not think the same way. People can get trapped into reacting and applying habitual patterns of deliberating based on their established mental model for thinking.

The expression "a closed mind" defines a fairly rigid and fixed view of the world, how it works, and what should be done. This frame of mind resists new approaches, thereby determining what people are willing to consider. Change does not come easy because issues fit into established categories and philosophical interpretations from the past.

The issue is how to listen with an open mind and to not always react in standard and habitual ways? Becoming aware of how one thinks and perceives life is necessary to understand how one makes sense of the communication: its philosophical and emotional foundation and intention.

To do so, Peter Senge and Otto Scharmer advocate "presencing," which is "being fully conscious and aware in the present moment. Then we began to appreciate presence as deep listening, of being open beyond one's preconceptions and historical ways of making sense. We came to see the importance of letting go of old identities and the need to control and . . . making choices to serve the evolution of life."[1]

Deep listening is temporarily suspending judgment and being willing to consider new information or points of view. Basically, it means listening and being receptive and considerate of the other person. Agreement is not required. Listen straightforwardly with respect for others. Simply trusting that what is said comes from the other person's beliefs and experience. Listeners must release any inner motivation and assumptions.

Presencing involves directing attention to possibilities. In many discussions, individuals assert a different view of the world and the future. When listening, presence is an absolute necessity—simply put, being in the present moment and concentrating all attention on the person and what is being said and not shutting down one's mind to different perspectives or distraction.

Presencing is a blended word combining sensing or feeling future possibilities and presence, the state of being present in the moment. When people pay attention, there is energy that follows that opens doors to really understanding and connecting with others.

Scharmer[2] believes that presencing requires close attention, which is a form of energy to open minds to what can unfold. The listener must observe, reflect, and explore options and the possible impact on the future.

Prejudgment closes doors. A person with a closed mind stifles the opportunity to think creatively. Suspending judgment and truly listening is critical; otherwise the conversation, in reality, is over before it begins—there is nothing new to explore or learn.

Another concern is the power to affect an individual's thinking by professional or social groups. Groupthink—going with the conventional, standard or social perspective censors any new thought or approach. Basically, it is going along with what the group or "conventional wisdom" contends. As Leo Tolstoy stated, "Wrong does not cease to be wrong because the majority shares it." Autocratic power surfaces when people let social or political groups determine their thinking. Standing up for one's beliefs is circumvented by social needs.

People conform to be accepted and not to be viewed as out of touch. In some cases, individuals fall into groupthink because of lack of self-confidence or fear of being isolated from the group. Social pressure on the Internet can create uniformity of perspective. Silos around politics and other issues are prevalent in part because individuals do not research contrary views and because much communication is tailored and restricted to short and terse comments.

In addition, listeners must reflect on their mental models and suppositions. There may be a better way to perceive and think about issues. To do so, however, one must understand their own mindset—how they perceive things philosophically and the knowledge they have about the subject. Independence in America's history refers to political liberty, as well as self-reliance and autonomy to determine the truth.

Mindfulness and listening simply mean to purposely pay attention, to be in the present, and not be judgmental. Being fully present and aware of one's own responses—emotionally and intellectually—ensures understanding the position of the person speaking and demonstrates consideration for him or her as a human being. Listening is intended to grasp the message, not simply frame a retort. This takes patience and curbing the desire to react instantly.

PEOPLE AND PERSONALITIES

Individuals think, feel, and behave differently: no two minds are the same. Some are extroverts (social butterflies or outgoing) and others are introverts (shy or nonconformists). Some are open or demonstrative, and others more closed or reserved. Some individuals are highly sensitive to comments, while there are others who are thick-skinned and immune to others' remarks or positions.

Throughout life's various circumstances, most people meet outgoing and cordial people, conscientious individuals, socially adept free spirits, introverted and quiet characters, or neurotic worriers anxious about life and events. People are aptly called individuals. Each person forms and molds their life because they have an exclusive combination of physical and personality characteristics, created through a distinctive history and character.

There are people who like to see facts and figures versus those who are instinctive and intuitive decision-makers. Some use only hard data, and others apply their emotions and instinct to direct their efforts. In many articles about leaders, they are characterized as individuals who are highly logical and follow their rational brains, while there may be others who follow their hearts and instinctive nature. At times, problems are such that both logic and heart are required: exceptional leaders are able to discern those circumstances. Many of them have to do with ethical values and morals and human needs.

Not everyone approaches issues or life the same, simply because they think differently. No one approach is better than the others, but different times or roles may call for distinct modes of thinking. Most individuals have confronted matters that require each approach.

Personality provides clues about the way individuals think. Some people are very logical and rational, and others perform very creatively and abstractly. At various times, people may use all of these approaches; however, some professions involve a particular type of thinking. Scientists require logical and rational processes, as do physicians and lawyers. They are evidence-driven through research and precedent: data and analysis are essential.

Analytical thinkers separate the whole into its component parts in order to determine their relationships. Logic, not emotion, is applied to find answers. Problems are restructured in a methodical way to address the question and define causes and responses.

Critical thinkers are quite logical in assessing and making judgments to determine authenticity and accuracy of proposals or ideas. Understanding how to make "the case" and judge things on their merit, using logic and analytics, are essential.

Obviously, writers, artists, and innovators perceive the world differently and apply nonlinear and more abstract perspectives. They interpret nature and life from a different and more unconventional and imaginative standpoint. They may be more astute and inspired to pursue new, exploratory or unorthodox paths.

Acting creatively and innovatively can be disruptive. Creativity and originality often are pursued with great passion. Many creative people are driven and relentless, while other individuals are simply interested in figuring out what they experience. Their thinking maybe unconventional and novel: they see and hear the world in different, creative ways.

Abstract thinkers are able to connect random things with each other. They see the big picture and search for meaning and interrelationships that elude others. Problem-solving is a role they enjoy: they perceive connections and the interplay of knowledge and concepts across content areas.

Those out-of-the-box creative thinkers, however, come up with imaginative ideas or solutions to solve problems or challenges. They find new approaches. Sometimes creative thinkers are not taken seriously because they can rattle and unnerve the status quo with their unique suggestions. Just consider how people eighty years ago would perceive today's communication technology and commerce. They probably would have scoffed if someone made that prediction.

On the other hand, there are the concrete thinkers: the opposite of the abstract ones. They like hard facts and figures and statistical analysis in their approach to thinking. Data must undergird the definition of problems, priorities, and responses. Emotion is restrained, and deduction and reasoning through statistics, data, and precedents are emphasized.

Some individuals are convergent thinkers who use a number of perspectives or concepts to find solutions. They define the various possibilities and conclude what they consider to be the best resolution. Divergent thinkers are the opposite. They explore an infinite number of solutions across content to find the one that is effective. They do not start off with a set number of possibilities, but instead conduct a far and wide search to find a solution.

MINDS

Many people assume that the brain and the mind are synonymous. They are not. The brain is a visible organ but the mind is not. In a sense, the brain is a receptacle—a physical place—where the mind resides. It is where the electronic impulses create thought.

The mind is where thinking happens: emotion, thought, memory, and imagination. Reason and logic are associated with the mind and the awareness and consciousness to control and understand what is happening and why. Comprehending the context and environment and adjusting to them is the work of the mind.

Everyone has a mind, but not all minds are the same. That is what makes conversations and dialogue interesting. Everyone has observed others and how their mind works. Some are able to logically plan to address circumstances, and there are others who perceive situations from a totally different and creative perspective. Some have the ability to understand the emotional and intangible modes and elements in a relationship or system—others do not.

Imagine a mind with the logical depth of a star computer engineer and the breadth and flexibility of a great saleswoman; with the rigor of a financial auditor and the improvisational skills of a master negotiator; with the capacity of a great private investigator to discern others' motives and strategies on the fly; with the discipline of a senior clinician at developing a comprehensive diagnosis of any ailment; with the nimbleness and emotional mobility of a seasoned actor and the vision of a master playwright. Would you not be setting out to cultivate and train such a mind if you are designing a program of study for a leader of the future?[3]

Certainly, this description defines a multitude of minds. With the various perspectives and skills required in these descriptions, it is hard to imagine any one individual being able to do everything that is stated and find meaning and satisfaction. These statements require different approaches to thinking—minds are the reservoirs of perspective and thought.

Not many people, if any, can really fit or fulfill the description above because each person has a different perspective, experience, and abilities. In a chaotic world, complex and tangled issues and problems arise that challenge society technologically and scientifically. Other matters raise social, psychological, and philosophical concerns and perspectives, as well as others.

Howard Gardner researched the various frames of mind and multiple intelligences. He cited that individuals have, to some extent, at least eight intelligences. They include the following:

- Linguistic—verbal ability
- Logical-mathematical—methods
- Spatial—use and manipulation of space
- Musical—perform and appreciate music
- Bodily/kinesthetic—the use of one's body
- Interpersonal—self-understanding of needs and emotions
- Intrapersonal—understanding of the needs and emotions of others
- Naturalist—ability to recognize and classify nature

Gardner disputes the idea that intelligence is a single property that can be measured on standardized tests. To him, intelligence is the "ability to solve problems, or create products, that are valued within one or more cultural settings."[4]

A related matter is the future—to analyze and deliberate about the changes that have taken place and to "see with new eyes" and not through the lens of the dogma or doctrine of the past. Today's world is far different from the one grandparents or great-grandparents experienced. However, one area—the application of the same ethics, principles, and values are applied to a changing society. Do different times mean different values, or do common values create a society that has commonalities—same ethic but different scenarios?

Being truthful, for example, was required in former times, as well as today and in the future.

Gardner in, *Five Minds for the Future*, identified that citizens will require the following: a disciplined mind, a respectful mind, a synthesizing mind, a creative mind, and an ethical mind. These categories not only involve thinking but also character.

The disciplined mind involves the basic literacy in the mastery of four disciplines: mathematics, science, history, and one art form. In addition, the study of ways of thinking is important.

A second is a synthesizing mind that can "knot together information from disparate sources into a coherent whole."[5] Reviewing past data, gathering new information, seeing connections, and knitting them together to determine its relevance to today.

The creative mind attempts new things through perception, cognitive processes and acquiring knowledge, but also by having a temperament and personality to risk failure and persevere. Failures are not a negative in this circumstance, but it takes persistence and resolves to continue. Failure is a part of life. The question is how to react to it.

Creativity requires a new mental perspective and the ability to review and determine whether or not it is relevant and purposeful. Artists and musicians and others see the world differently and provide new and innovative interpretations and perspectives.

In all relationships in society, respect is an imperative. A respectful mind assumes that diversity is positive and a reality in which each individual merits respect. The world is interconnected and requires understanding and civility to bring divergent people—in all forms—together. Diversity is more than race or ethnicity. It involves thinking and philosophy: how people see the world and society and the approaches that can be applied.

The ethical mind requires individuals to think for themselves and recognize the rights and responsibilities of others. A prerequisite for an ethical society and relationships is understanding values and principles. Most individuals admire good work and desire ethical treatment of themselves and others. Ethics and principles establish norms for the treatment of individuals personally, as well as socially and politically. The individual is concerned with proper principled behavior.

MINDSETS

A mindset is a fixed disposition affecting and directing responses and behavior. It reflects the attitude, ideas, and values that determine how individuals respond. Many times a person's initial reaction to another person is shaped by their mindset, which may be open, closed, or uncertain. People have a mind of their own. Not everyone perceives things the same way or reacts in the same manner.

Individuals' minds shape their lives and actions and reactions. Their philosophical and practical disposition affects their impressions and actions. They help individuals make sense of the world and what they feel, do, and think. As individuals speak, the listeners are unconsciously applying their mindset to what is stated. Mindsets are a filtering and interpretive agent of the communication's content and intent.

Mindsets are basically a frame of mind—thoughts and beliefs that form ones thinking habits and reactions. They can be thought of as habits of the mind: those beliefs and attitudes affecting self-perception and how the world around them works. Reactions, as well as perspective, emerge from seeing and hearing the world through one's mindset.

Beliefs—based on experience, knowledge, or philosophy—shape mindsets. Attitudes are an established way of perceiving and feeling about issues, ideas, or people. They can be open and positive or closed and negative. Immediate responses of individuals emanate from their mindset. In addition, people may not be self-aware of their own mindset.

Mindsets can be a negative filter and create blind spots about how to look at the world and events. A closed mind results from one's mindset. Understanding may be shallow, and painful past experiences may not reflect contemporary circumstances. Losses and failures often live within one's mind and are resurrected in times of risk or difficulty.

Mindsets affect relationships with others, as well as an individual's beliefs about himself or herself. Each individual has a self-image of him or herself that establishes what each individual thinks of him or herself in the present and future. A person's mindset affects self-perception and role in the world and determines whether they become the person they can or want to be.

Carol Dweck, in her book *Mindset*, discusses the impact of the minds people adopt: she indicates there are two basic mindsets—fixed and growth. Dweck asserts that some individuals believe their qualities are rigid—carved in stone. These individuals believe their intelligence is fixed and that their personality and moral character are determined and will not change. However, Dweck indicates that mindsets are beliefs that can change because people have a choice. Ability, for example, is not fixed. It can change through learning.

Too often, people think their abilities and skills are set in concrete and cannot be changed. They believe that intelligence, character, and creativity are determined and may not be modified or improved. What they have is what they have. Conscious of their fixed nature, they feel compelled to prove themselves over and over again. Consequently, avoiding failure at all costs verifies "every situation calls for confirmation of their intelligence, personality, or character. Every situation is evaluated: Will I succeed or fail? Will I look smart or dumb? Will I be accepted or rejected? Will I feel like a winner or loser."[6] Growth is not on this person's radar—success and proving worth, not development, is.

A growth mindset, on the other hand, is based on the premise that one's abilities, talents, and perspectives can be improved and cultivated. A person's potential is unknown and can be expanded and tapped through education and commitment. Consequently, hard work and perseverance matter because talent and skill can be developed. Failure is not feared because it can be the reservoir for examining beliefs and talents and growth.

A passion for learning is a part of maturing and tackling new opportunities and events. Ability is not static: everyone can grow and advance. People with growth mindsets perceive themselves as being able to learn and refine their talents and skills.

The fixed and growth mindsets also influence the view of the world and others. Fixed mindsets perceive the world as a place where success comes from proving oneself to be smart and talented. In a growth mindset, it is about learning and stretching oneself and facing challenges without the certainty of success.

LISTENING MINDSET

Besides the context in which it is taking place, mindsets affect how well listening occurs and its impact on both the speaker and the listener. As in many situations, a positive virtue can become a problem.

Take passion. Individuals may be passionate about the subject matter in a conversation or presentation. That certainly opens the door to listen, but it can also be a problem. Passion, while raising interest and energy, can also be blown into arrogance by the inability to respectfully listen and to continually interrupt and speak. Toning down passion is not always easy, but a dose of empathy for the speakers allows them to make their points.

Another virtue that can get in the way is the penchant to problem solve for others. Too often, individuals proclaim solutions or pathways before the individual has finished the presentation. This can be very distracting, and the issue at hand may not be fully or clearly expressed. There are times when individuals offer solutions to a problem that was not part of the discussion because they rushed judgment and did not totally listen. Incomplete information or misinterpretation leads to errors, and the credibility of the listener is compromised. Patience as a listener in this case and not rushing to judgment or solving a perceived problem is the best course.

Sometimes chaos reigns at home, in the workplace, or certainly in politics that heightens emotions. The response is usually to present a solution or debate based on an individual's mindset of the situational world. Asking better questions, and listening and understanding substance and intent are requisites. Quality questions require thought. The so-called "gotcha" question is distractive because, in many cases, it is supposed to discredit the speaker and not clarify the issue or present more information.

A listening mindset is geared to truly comprehending the ideas, concepts, information, and philosophy in the discussion. Simply stated, the listener should be able to accurately repeat back what the speaker stated and define its meaning accurately. To the speaker, knowing that he or she was understood builds trust that the listener is consciously attentive and present. In listening to others, determining what is opinion and what is knowledge is essential. Philosopher Mortimer Adler stated: "Let us return to the focal point of this discussion—the distinction between knowledge and mere opinion. On the one hand, we have self-evident truths that have certitude and incorrigibility; and we also have truths that are still subject to doubt but are supported by evidence and reasons to a degree that puts them in beyond reasonable doubt or at least gives them predominance over contrary views. All else is mere opinion—with no claim to being knowledge or having any hold on truth."[7]

Adler describes self-evident truths as those that state something the opposite of which is impossible to think. For example, the finite whole is larger than any of its parts. A part cannot be larger than the whole.

Some things can be claimed to be true on the basis of evidence and reasons that are available now, but turn out to be false in the future. New evidence that comes into play can revise what was taken as a truth in prior times. For example, the Earth is the center of the universe or the Great Wall of China can be seen from outer space. Obviously, Earth is not the center, and it is pretty hard to pick out the Great Wall of China from any space-based locale. It is built from rocks collected from all over the local landscape; consequently, they are usually the same color as the wall itself. In the low earth orbit, the wall can be seen.

Listeners and speakers make choices based on their emotions and frame of mind. Mindsets! Some of these choices are made automatically without deep thought like driving a car. Individuals in today's society need to develop an evaluative mindset that includes reflecting on defining assumptions and theories. In presentations and discussions, analyzing positions and conclusions require deeper thought than in casual conversations.

Listening requires concentration and thought to comprehend and find meaning, process information, and understand the philosophy and emotions behind the speaker's positions. Listening requires patience and, at times, a bit of courage to hear and interpret a person's message and point of view. It is much more than silence.

NOTES

1. Senge, *Presence*, Loc 230, Kindle.

2. Otto Scharmer and Katrin Kaufer, *Leading from the Emerging Future: From Ego-System to Eco-System Economies* (Barrett-Kohler Publishers, 2013), Kindle.

3. Mihnea Moldoveanu and Roger Martin, *Diaminds: Decoding the Mental Habits of Successful Thinkers* (Toronto: University of Toronto Press, 2010), 3.

4. Howard Gardner, *Frames of Mind* (New York: Basic Books, 1993), x.

5. Howard Gardner, *Five Minds of the Future* (Boston: Harvard Business Press, 2008), 46.

6. Carol S. Dweck, *Mindset* (New York: Ballantine Books, 2008), 6.

7. Mortimer J. Adler, *Ten Philosophical Mistakes* (Touchstone, 1997), 99–100, Kindle.

Chapter 9

Thinking

We cannot solve problems by using the same kind of thinking we used when we created them.

—Albert Einstein

The essence of immorality is the tendency to make an exception of myself.

—Jane Addams

Children are told to think before they react. When things go awry, parents will ask, "What were you thinking?" The concern is that not thinking is the problem that can create issues and have devastating effects. Children are not the only ones that need to learn a lesson.

History has many examples of brilliant thinkers. Great ideas brought forth ideologies that were the foundation for democratic governments, social systems, and principles that improved healthcare, communication, governance, and other aspects of life.

Of course, history has demonstrated the other side of movements that promoted corrupt cultural, scientific, and political policies that degraded institutions and segments of the population. Some of these movements were not only factually wrong but also morally corrupt and reprehensible.

Most communication efforts are aimed at trying to get others to change. Some individuals arrogantly think they know what is best for everyone; that they are smarter than others and their roles are is to enlighten them. Acclaimed leaders are not always the best; they often appeal to people's emotions, fears, and prejudices. The issue is that in groups people will accept illogical belief systems and ideologies because of peers or the need for acceptance.

Diversity of perspective and thought are not always seen as a virtue. Sometimes people come to discussions with arrogant and egocentric perspectives: they want their thinking accepted and validated, and they want to be perceived as bright and right. Often, the result is rigidity in thought. Collaborating with each other is scuttled, and parties with different views are perceived not as opponents or those with an independent perspective or philosophy, but as enemies. Thinking stops, derision begins, superiority reins, and communication halts.

Linda Elder[1] indicates that people engage in social-centric thinking. Simply stated: "Our group is the best." Elitist perspectives carve the population into know-nothings versus elites who think they grasp how the world and culture should work and what is right and needs to be done. This can occur in small social groups or in political and government promotions. People go along with the crowd. Individuals must review their own reasoning and assumptions to determine whether they are justifiable. If they do not, they miss other more reasonable points of view and possible implications—both upsides and downsides.

In these circumstances, "junk thought" can prevail, which involves "anti-rationalization and contempt for countervailing facts and expert opinion."[2] Often the language of science and technology is used to frame "junk thought" and make it more palatable and acceptable—statistics and numerical data are used or facts are "cherry picked" to make the position seem more accurate. At times, speakers use statistics repeatedly because people see them as scientific and without error.

To counter this, rational and critical thinking is essential to determine if conclusions make sense and are derived from valid studies and sources. Doing so requires some understanding of statistics and, in addition, the concepts of research design. Logic along with analytical and divergent thinking is necessary. Research must be valid and based on proper procedures to ensure its credibility and legitimacy.

Arguments and points of view should make sense and be upheld by evidence. Critical thinking is necessary to determine if research and the line of reasoning are clear, accurate, and relevant. Opposing perspectives should be presented and done so in good faith: What is the counter position? Is the position or recommendation essential and significant or is it of little note? Another issue is unintended consequences. What are the possible reverberations and byproducts of policies and proposals? All recommendations have some problematic concerns. They are a part of all decisions, including those individuals support. Thoughtful people will always give this consideration in order to ensure a greater possibility of success.

The other issue is whether or not there is a vested interest in the recommendations and programs. Is it fair and are opposing views presented fairly?

Has the content been presented ethically and honestly, or is it one-sided and geared to the interests of special interests. In some cases, solutions are offered with the impression that there is no other choice. Sometimes, doing nothing is a correct decision: this is a more difficult decision than people realize.

Reviewing issues from an idealistic perspective is important. What is proposed may be contrary to the goals and values of the person and organization and may raise questions. Finally, pragmatism comes into play, which simply means finding the most effective approach to meeting values and ideals.

COLLABORATION AND UNDERSTANDING

When people are committed to getting things done, collaboration is essential. In any democratic institution, different viewpoints and perspectives are evident and proposed. To get things done, working with people who differ is vital to finding a path forward.

Adam Kahane advocates "stretch collaboration" that shifts the way groups work by embracing the conflict and the connection with the "team."[3] The group considers and experiments systematically with different perspectives and possibilities. Finally, individuals must "stretch" away from trying to change others and to enter into the "action" and change themselves—to look inside and be open to other viewpoints, which can result in creative solutions. People learn to open different perspectives.

Kahane believes individuals must move away from one plan and examine other options or possibilities. Working with others with diverse viewpoints is challenging and not always easy or straightforward. Energy exists, both positive and negative, and the pathway is diverse and complex. Moving ahead without fear, but with their interpersonal connection and awareness, can produce results. Dialogue is one possible approach. Patience, no matter the approach, is indispensable because collaboration takes time. There is no magic wand.

The Socratic method is sometimes viewed as questioning everything. In a sense, the Socratic method is intended to think critically by understanding the individual's beliefs and rationale, and discerning whether or not they make sense. Questions are asked in a respectful and focused way to learn what individuals mean by what they say and why they think the way they do. This involves reasoning and determining the basis and implications of their points of view. Being an empathetic listener requires a genuine interest in the other individual's perspective and encounters, as well as findings. Being open to another's position is much different than reacting emotionally to preconceptions.

Good listeners do not interrupt—they simply allow the person to express themselves without interference. Listening carefully—not framing comments or arguments in response—allows the speaker to complete their thought.

Conversations are not about judging, criticizing, or correcting others. Actually, they should deepen connections and relationships through understanding and empathy, and a genuine interest in people's perspective and how they arrived at it.

THOUGHT

Thinking is the foundation for listening. People associate thought with the brain and as simply a cognitive exercise: a unitary activity of the brain. Physicist David Bohm in his book, *Thought as a System*, has a more comprehensive view. He believed: "That body, emotion, intellect, reflex and artifact are now understood as one unbroken field of mutually informing thought. All of these components interpenetrate one another to such an extent . . . that we are compelled to see 'thought as a system.'"[4]

Bohm asserted that thought is not just about the present, because the past carries into the present through feelings, both pleasurable and painful ones. Thought leads to creating meaning, which is interconnected to the process of thinking. Individuals' meaning is dependent upon their system of thinking.

Bohm goes on to say,

> Let's look at this question of meaning. The dictionary gives three senses of the word "meaning." One of them is "significance"; it's like a "sign" that points to something. Another is "value." And there is "purpose" or "intention." These are connected, because if you say "something means a lot to me," you mean it has a high value. And if you say "I mean to do it," that is the same as to say "it's my purpose, my intention." They're related words, obviously. Something with great significance will generate a sense of value. And the value is the energy that infuses you; it makes you feel it's worth doing, or worthwhile.[5]

What is of significance depends on one's thoughts. Consequently, people perceive meaning and relevance in different ways, affecting their emotions and perceptions, as well as their analysis and action. Determining fact or fiction is based on their assumptions and values. That is why two people listening to the same presentation can come to different conclusions.

Finding shared meaning is important in relationships and societies. Diversity of thought is related to the diversity of experience, emotions, and philosophy. Interpreting things in life is acting out the patterns and thoughts residing in memory. Thoughts and feelings are powerful because of their connection to the past events and mindsets. Values and perspectives develop through knowledge and experience.

Unusual or new circumstances may require different and innovative responses, not simply acting out a pattern, which can be restrictive. New circumstances bring tension and anxiety because past perceptions can be limiting, personally and socially. At times, a fresh frame of mind is necessary: jumping to conclusions can be quite negative because the past and the present circumstances are not exactly the same.

TYPES OF THINKING

Aristotle identified three types of thinking that affect human activity: simply described as "making, doing, and knowing."

"Makers" are artists or artisans who produce all sorts of things—shoes, ships, art, and music. "Doers" are moral and social beings who want to do what they are compelled to do to find happiness and meaning. "Knowers," people who are learners, require knowledge of all sorts including about knowledge itself.

According to Adler, Aristotle was concerned with the differences that distinguish the various kinds of thinking. "He used the term 'productive thinking' to describe the kind of thinking that man engages in as a maker; 'practical thinking' to describe the kind that he engages in as a doer; and 'speculative' or 'theoretical thinking' to describe the kind he engages in as a knower."[6] Some of Aristotle's books on moral and political philosophy concern man as a practical doer: living life and trying to make it as good as possible. His books on natural philosophy concern theoretical thinking and man's mind, views, and knowledge of the world.

People do not think or perceive the world the same way. There is no one type of thinking. Many individuals believe that everyone thinks the same way—in the same pattern. That, however, is not the reality. The reason why perspectives and conclusions differ among people is the way they think. An artist and a lawyer may view the issues and life in different ways because of how they approach thinking. Scientists and artists approach it differently, and philosophers and code developers address issues in distinct fashion.

Artists embrace uncertainty and unique perceptions. They often see what is unmentioned, are curious, and see opportunities and take action. Creative people daydream, observe, question, listen, and are intrinsically motivated. Failure is not a deterrent because they accept circumstances and ambiguity and reframe things. In art, there is no one correct interpretation or outcome: there are a variety of nuances. Beauty and interpretation are not always tangible or concrete, and imagination thrives with those who think beyond what they tangibly see.

Scientists, on the other hand, ask questions, observe, and study, collecting tangible evidence and data through research and testing, sometimes repeatedly. They design and perform experiments to answer questions and test hypotheses. They use reason and analysis to challenge assumptions, responses, and answers. They are skeptical and want to find the concrete truth. Finding the truth and adding to the literature and knowledge base is a driving force.

Lawyers think carefully and precisely on legal questions. "Making the case," legal principles and values, and defining the truth are their major roles. Legal minds are able to make arguments on both sides of an issue or question; they exercise judgment and combine realism with idealism. The basis is legal concepts and philosophical thought about the principles of life, liberty, and the pursuit of happiness. Situations, actions, and outcomes in a civil society are based on legal concepts and democratic values.

Analytical thinking is necessary: lawyers must make the case on all sides of the question in order to be successful in representing a position. Answering a somewhat elusive concept or question "what is justice?" is their role in life circumstances. They deal with pragmatic, philosophical, and abstract questions concerning the law and justice. Discerning the truth on moral or legal questions is imperative. How do things stack up to legal concepts, and interpretations and precedents? Lawyers must know their audience, their case, and their adversary's position. They proceed methodically and don't overstate their case to demonstrate the merits of their position and the defects of their adversary.[7]

Others, such as executives and other leaders, must deal with hard data, philosophical aspirations, and human relationships, which occur in a chaotic world of tangibles and intangibles. Strategic and reflective thinking in a focused and results-oriented manner must take place, often with teams and committees. There are knowns and unknowns in questions and problems.

Thinking in this framework requires tangible data, but also perceptual knowledge and, at times, intuition. The world does not always operate based on pure reason and logic: emotions present real issues also. Leaders comprehend and understand the intangibles that commit and drive individuals to a cause, sometimes beyond well-reasoned and sensible approaches. Intuition can direct action, beyond time-honored ways or the views of the majority.

In all these examples and others, the approach to thinking is quite different. They include the following:

• Concrete thinking versus abstract thinking
• Convergent thinking versus divergent thinking

- Creative thinking versus analytical thinking
- Sequential (linear thinking) versus holistic thinking

In brief, concrete thinking concerns comprehending and applying information. Divergent thinkers have the ability to generate creative ideas by bringing facts and data together and applying logic and knowledge to solve problems.

Convergent thinkers collect facts and data from a variety of sources and apply logic and knowledge to solve problems, gather bits of information, and put the pieces together to come to a conclusion. Emergent thinking involves breaking a topic into its corollary pieces and exploring the various parts, and then generating new ideas and solutions.

Analytical thinkers separate information into its component parts and review and examine the relationships in a step-by-step process to analyze and solve problems. Critical thinkers develop new and innovative ideas by reviewing thoughts, theories, and procedures to determine what is reasonable or unreasonable.

Finally, sequential thinkers process information in an orderly prescribed manner step-by-step or part-to-whole. While holistic thinkers see the big picture and define the interconnections of the component parts of the system—whole-to-part.

THINKING AND LISTENING

Speaker's and listener's approaches to digesting and presenting information are defined by their thinking process, which affects their perspective and attitude. Obviously, emotion influences how people think and react. In crisis situations, individuals can forsake their usual approaches and become untethered because of the power of emotions. Those who see the larger picture and the chaos around it may respond less emotionally and more linearly in the unfolding confusion and uncertainty—they do not panic.

Thinking raises questions and concepts and also examines assumptions and implications. Determining the point of view of the message is a major aspect of this process. Where is the person coming from factually, pragmatically, and philosophically? Listening thoroughly includes defining the logic behind the person's presentation. Does the position make sense, and does it have a reasoned basis for pragmatic or philosophical implementation? Are the facts and data logical and relevant?

Speakers and listeners must both apply thinking skills. Just as presenters use different thinking approaches—concrete, abstract, convergent, divergent, creative, analytical, sequential, or holistic—listeners also use these approaches in comprehending and reacting to the presentation or circumstances. However, not everyone is skilled in the various approaches to thinking.

An artist speaking to a group of research scientists about the subject of truth might have a totally different reaction than when speaking to peers. Are art and beauty subjective in expressing a point of view? The same is true for scientists to examine artists' mindsets and philosophies. Both parties may have different perspectives on the subject of truth and on what is objective and subjective because of the nature of their work.

At times, conflicts exist between science and propositions or opinions. In science, there are self-evident truths that are proven through the scientific method and research that is sustained through other studies to ensure credibility. Without these foundations, Adler states, "All else is mere opinion—with no claim to being knowledge or having any hold on truth."[8]

THOUGHT AND MORALITY

A philosophical question exists about whether information is based on genuine knowledge or matters of interpretation. Some argue that judgments about moral values are open to opinion—good and evil, and right and wrong, for example. Others believe that they are simply preferences or beliefs. And, some may say, "It depends!" Philosophers argue this point and how they think about it.

Parents wish for a good life for their children, which is not simply about money or status. In many ways, it is more about character—living and acting based on principles, values, and morals. Honor and self-esteem are a part of making "good" choices. Honor, in this case, is standing for and living positive values: making the right choices, which is a matter of virtue. Matters of soul, happiness, and making "good" choices are involved.

Society is based on autonomy and choice. This raises, at times, the conflict between what is personally advantageous and what is in the best interest of creating a "good" society and community. The immediate pushes decision-making, rather than a higher good that may take more time. Some decisions have to be made immediately (safety and emergencies), but others do not. Attending to special interests can curtail pursuing the greater good for many. Pressure of self-image or special interests can cause individuals to decide quickly, sacrificing prudence for the appearance of decisiveness.

Thought is critically important in decisions about the standards by which one lives life. Individuals are taught to think before they act because the repercussions can be immense. But what about not thinking? Yes, not thinking! Does that really happen? Do people just comply without examining consequences morally, socially, or personally?

Political philosopher Hanna Arendt went to Jerusalem for the Adolf Eichmann trial and wrote a controversial article for the New Yorker magazine. She stated that "the longer one listened to him, the more obvious it became that his inability to speak was closely connected with an inability to *think*; that is, to think from the standpoint of somebody else."[9] She added,

He was not stupid. It was sheer thoughtlessness—something by no means identical with stupidity—that predisposed him to become one of the greatest criminals of that period. And if this is "banal" and even funny, if with the best will in the world one cannot extract any diabolical or demonic profundity from Eichmann, that is still far from calling it commonplace.[10]

Arendt's argument is that Eichmann was not some demonic character—he was a morally vacuous and shallow person who did not think, but simply did what he was told. In less formal parlance, groupthink and not thinking critically, or certainly from a moral standpoint, can have dire consequences. Evil occurs because individuals do not think analytically or comprehensively, no less from a moral and ethical position.

Extreme decadence occurred in the past because in the face of authority, people became compliant. Moral choices, however, are still the prerogative of each individual, however, with the risk in autocratic circumstances of reprisal. Citizens in democracies have to think and to stand on principle, and not just "do their job" and comply, and go along.

Behaving thoughtlessly occurs when adherence to clichés and socially accepted norms of behavior are followed without examining their origin, impact, or moral standing. Some people say, "Who is to judge?" But history illustrates that each citizen must judge and not be curtailed by social or political pressure or expectations.

Doing one's duty does not excuse immoral behavior if the duty results in immoral consequences. Thinking and questioning are necessary for all aspects of life, along with courage to stand on moral principles personally or in civic and social life. These are difficult circumstances.

Each individual has an inner voice that pushes one's conscience to review expectations and behavior. In society, people cannot thoughtlessly accept the standards or expectations of the larger society without reflection and deep thought. Being thoughtless and swept up by political, social, or other group's doctrine and not thinking of the personal values and mores is nothing more than being a "sheep" going along with the flock, which can lead to minor indiscretions or huge societal calamities as history has demonstrated.

At times, thinking pushes individuals to be the "wolf howling in the wilderness," asserting the truth and justice against the accepted or conventional position necessary for a good society. Every person, within their own mind, has an idea of the kind of person they want to be based on values, ethics, and aspirations. Social and political authoritarian groups push for group thought, not individual values or principles of truth, beauty, justice, or liberty. People have choices and they can think. As Jean-Paul Sartre supposedly said, "We are our choices."

Essayist E. B. White stated, "One need only watch totalitarians at work to say that once men gain power over other men's minds, that power is never used sparingly and wisely, but lavishly and with unspeakable results."[11]

NOTES

1. Linda Elder, "Become a Critical Thinker," The head of the Foundation for Critical Thinking, Interview by Karen Christensen: The necessary revolution in the way we think, http://www.forbesindia.com/interview/rotman/become-a-critical-thinker/26592/1.

2. Susan Jacoby, *The Age of American Unreason* (New York: Vintage Books, 2009), 211.

3. Adam Kahane, *Collaborating with the Enemy: How to Work with People You Don't Agree With or Like or Trust* (Berrett-Koehler Publishers, 2017), Loc 262–75, Kindle.

4. David Bohm, *Thought as a System* (Taylor and Francis, 2004), Loc 69, Kindle.

5. Bohm, *Thought as a System*, Loc 2744.

6. Bohm, *Thought as a System*, 17.

7. Antonin Scalia and Bryan A. Gardner, *Making Your Case* (St. Paul, MN: Thompson/West, 2008), 13.

8. Adler, *Ten Philosophical Mistakes*, 100.

9. Hanna Arendt, *Eichmann in Jerusalem: A Report on the Banality of Evil* (Penguin Publishing Group, 2006), Loc 1125, Kindle.

10. Arendt, *Eichmann in Jerusalem*, 5024.

11. E. B. White, *On Democracy* (New York: HarperCollins, 2019), 74.

Chapter 10

People

A human being is a part of the whole, called by us the universe. A part limited in time and space. He experiences himself, his thoughts and feeling as something separate from the rest, a kind of optical delusion of his consciousness. This delusion is a kind of prison for us, restricting us to our personal desires and to affection for a few persons nearest to us. Our task must be to free ourselves from this prison by widening our circle of compassion to embrace all living creatures.

—Albert Einstein

Courage is the measure of our heartfelt participation with life, with another, with a community, a work; a future.

—David Whyte

The pace of life has accelerated, and time passes without really knowing and appreciating others. Face-to-face conversations or simply sitting quietly together get lost in the ventures of career success and the intrusion of social distractions and materialism. People can lose the "being" of life: togetherness, closeness, and fellowship that enriches life and its significance. The human heart and emotions bind people together.

While the availability of technology and other tools are clearly evident, relationships can become more superficial and less personal. Deep feelings and friendships are more than e-mails and tweets: being together person-to-person opens individuals to truly share themselves.

Person-to-person connections, whether it be with friends, family, or lovers, require the ability to share who they are as human beings, not as a job title or other descriptor. As society becomes more technically focused, human attachment can dissolve as individuals withdraw within themselves because presence is absent.

The result is that families and society become disconnected because a technological screen does not really convey a person's full being and energy. The simple needs of being truly together—listening, helping, and loving—simply disappear into the hackneyed allure of technology. True feelings are not addressed, and disengagement occurs. As Norman Cousins stated, "An individual is capable of great compassion and great indifference."[1] Without physical presence, communication fades into cognitive exchanges and is not the same personally as human presence and touch.

Individuals have minds and emotions, but they also have a social inner self and identity that influences their needs and decisions. Integrity to oneself is a part of soulful activity and is reflected in one's genuineness, his or her essence and moral fiber and beliefs. Soulful activity or responses concern compassion, sensitivity, and honesty in relationships, and are true indications of interconnection and care.

Nobleness not in the sense of aristocracy but in the consideration and caring treatment of others is more important than words. Being righteous and generous matters in relationships with people. Concern with and for others originates from this sense. Everyone desires to be understood and respected by others, and communication is the means to an honest and deep, heartfelt bond.

NEED FOR CONNECTION

Friends are important to people because they provide perspective and insight into life and its path, struggles, and successes. In dark times, they are a safe harbor and a person to sit with in the silence of grief or failure. Empathy and consideration in these, as well as happy times, dissolves loneliness, as friendship and togetherness unfold.

People feel that they are not alone: that they are linked, not for any mercenary purposes, but simply for their emotional and intellectual well-being. Loneliness and isolation can be destructive. Relationships move people beyond self-absorption and living within themselves.

Meeting these needs in most cases evolves through relationships with others. According to research, about 70 percent of a person's day is spent in interpersonal communication, and 45 percent of that 70 percent is spent listening. Listening is powerful for both speakers and listeners. Everyone needs to be understood and to be respected and appreciated. Agreement is not necessary for a respectful relationship to develop. Great friends often have different ideas or philosophies, but they respect and love their counterparts.

The Department of Labor Statistics[2] revealed that 46 percent of those who quit their jobs did so because they were not listened to, and therefore, they felt unappreciated, which is a larger issue than simply being heard. Indifference is contrary to the need to connect in relationships at home, work, and the larger society.

The need for self-respect and for the esteem of others is related to love. Esteem stems from achievement and capability; strength and confidence in facing challenges, surviving, and succeeding. Reputation and prestige are an aspect of recognition and appreciation from others. Fulfillment of these needs leads to self-confidence and competence. Many people expect their needs to be fulfilled through their work or other organizations.

Being understood is one of those issues that builds or destroys relationships and trust. It is one of the most personal connections between two people because it involves not only ideas or cognitive impressions but also heartfelt feelings. Sharing one's soul and opening up to another person is far beyond expressing simple opinions. Feelings of sadness, anxiety, loss, hope, joy, and love are highly personal and revealing. To share these with another individual requires a high level of trust and confidence.

Speaking and being heard are important aspects of both belongingness and self-respect. Being truly heard and recognized reduces or lowers the impact of difficult feelings. Expressing emotions is only safe if one person trusts another. Having someone understand requires not only comprehending the words and circumstance but also grasping the sincere feelings behind them. Realizing why people feel as they do is at the root of acknowledging their story and message. Sharing in this manner requires not only understanding thoughts, but also emotions and attitudes.

Heartfelt conversations are deeper and richer than simply voicing opinions or ideas. In these conversations, no one has to propose a remedy or take responsibility for the issue or emotion. Helping in most situations simply means understanding the conditions and emotional aspects of circumstances and showing care.

The listener can use "I" statements in these situations, which simply is a tool to clarify the substance and feelings in the conversation. An "I" statement, for example, is: "I sense that you . . . ," "I understand that . . ." or "I hear you say . . ." These statements open doors to both the feelings and substance of the speaker. They help eliminate distractions or confusion and clarify the feelings and ideas the speaker is trying to express. "I" statements help eliminate distractions so that there is a true understanding of the speaker's point of view and attitude.

"I" statements can be used by the speaker to the listener as well. For example, if the speaker feels that the listener is not listening, he or she can state, "I feel that my concerns are not being heard," rather than "I feel you're not listening to me now."

An "I" statement basically indicates how the circumstances look from the listener's or speaker's perspective. It is not meant to blame; it is simply an expression of how they react to the presentation. Reflecting and paraphrasing are indicators that the speaker is heard correctly in terms of substance and impact.

At times, listening must reinforce what others feel. Statements such as "that must have been very difficult for you" address feelings and emotions. This may open up the person to share feelings behind the messages' content. Authentically acknowledging one's own feelings and finding common ground can be the result.

If people do not feel heard, several outcomes surface. Speakers begin to talk faster and louder for fear of being interrupted. Conversely, some may intentionally speak quietly, so others have to pay greater attention to hear their words. Repeating oneself is also an indication that they do not feel the proper attention is being paid to them or the issue at hand. In other situations, people will just turn off and not say anything because they feel it is worthless and a waste of time.

DIFFICULT CONVERSATIONS

Parents, adults, leaders, and others have to confront tough conversations at times. Often these are avoided because of wanting to evade possible conflict. Not confronting them diminishes relationships. and clarity and honest engagement are lost. The idea is not to shame or to blame, but to help individuals, teams, and families function more effectively in meeting their goals.

Engaging the difficult conversations takes courage to be there and address the issues. Values and aspirations require the ability to address circumstances or problems that are impeding them. Raising issues and listening with an open heart to the perspectives of others is important. It is not a discussion of winning or losing, but one to define and provide feedback and what is needed for improvement and success.

Difficult conversations convey what occurred, the feelings involved, and what the situation means to everyone. Any bad news should be given up front. In the circumstances, there will be things that cannot be changed and those that can. Blaming is not the goal, but finding a means for everyone to address the issue is. Emotions can be a part of the discussion, and some may respond negatively.

Individuals, however, often resist truth about themselves. That is not unusual. Abraham Maslow stated, "More than any other kind of knowledge we fear knowledge of ourselves, knowledge that might transform our self-esteem and our self-image."[3] Examining oneself in answering the question "who am I?" requires dissolving any fear of the truth about oneself. Being truly self-reflective requires listening to others' perceptions—particularly those who do it with care and love.

In these conversations, everyone must genuinely listen and must summarize and paraphrase what they heard. Summarizing is important. Problem-solving can then begin.

AUTHENTIC COMMUNICATION

Authenticity in all forms of communication is necessary for individuals to trust and believe the person. Otherwise, no one will rely on the accuracy of the message because truthfulness will be questioned. Listeners will not engage openly—information or emotion—if the speaker is not or does not appear to be authentic.

Authenticity relates not only to content of communication but also to emotions. Sometimes emotions are not expressed sincerely but are disingenuous. Genuine emotions are authentic and true to the person's demeanor and actual feelings. Openness is vitally important in the relationship between speaker and listener. In any relationship whether at work or personally everyone wants to be understood: what they are saying and why.

Communication opens the door to learning. Learning actually starts when people listen to one another rather than talk at or past each other. Listening is not easy and requires looking inward and being aware of mindsets, biases, and limitations of the speaker and listener. Placing ego aside is necessary to compassionately understand another person's feelings and interpretations.

In conversations, each individual has an interior dialogue with themselves as well as a discussion with others. Open-mindedness is required to move toward deeper listening and engaging in authentic conversations. Both speaker and listener must reflect and be open to each other and must be vulnerable to learning and growing. If this happens, then a feeling of mutual trust as well as a true connection is established.

NOTES

1. Norman Cousins, *Human Options* (New York: W. W. Norton and Company, 1981), 58.

2. Howick Associates, *Listening Statistics*, Blog, https://b2b.kununu.com/blog/why-do-good-employees-quit-leave-their-job.

3. Maslow, *The Psychology of Science*, 16.

Epilogue

Wisdom and Honor

I also often ask my guests about what they consider to be their invisible weaknesses and shortcomings. I do this because these are the characteristics that define us no less than our strengths. What we feel sets us apart from other people is often the thing that shapes us as individuals.

—Terry Gross, *NPR Fresh Air*

Words are events, they do things, change things. They transform both speaker and hearer; they feed energy back and forth and amplify it. They feed understanding or emotion back and forth and amplify it.

—Ursula LeGuin

Moving through life opens doors to the heart and mind. Emotion and reason appeal to all aspects of human existence. Sometimes, they both are in harmony, and at other times, they are dissonant. The impassioned heart will sometimes negate the surge of rational judgment—"I know I shouldn't pursue this, but I feel in my heart . . . ." At other times, the mind subdues the heartfelt emotion and rallies action based on reason and logic. "I'd love to try it, but I can't take risk because."

The heart and mind skirmish when significant consequences are on the line: in other words, what is best in the long run, family, ambition, dreams, finances, or mission.

When business executive, Claire, left her job in Chicago to move to Boston to marry Jack, she did so out of emotion. She left the pending promotion and a large increase in salary to be with a teacher in a small public school.

Reasonable? Does it emotionally overpower the reasoned certainty of better career opportunities? Should she delay committing to a marriage after eight years in the relationship to pursue a highly regarded promotion?

Heart and mind present perspectives that are important to be considered. In either of the situations mentioned, was there really a right or wrong answer? What if Claire took the promotion and career opportunities that had great professional and financial potential? Will love prevail or will accepting a significant professional position take precedence? These are difficult decisions based on the individual's life and needs: love or aspirations?

Thinking in these situations is complex. Issues of short-term and long-term consequences are involved. Both Claire and Jack must not be silent. They both have to discuss the situation. Staying silent is a recipe for discord later on—blaming the other person for "sacrificing" his or her career or life for the other.

Communication in relationships is an absolute necessity because decisions concern more than one person, and the decision of this magnitude has consequences in all facets of the relationship. After all, relationships grow or wilt if they are not "together" on the decision. If one or the other decided to "do it for you," it can raise difficulties long term. Clear communication of values, fears, and limits must be discussed between them.

In difficult times, such as wars and quarantines, people understand the need for communication and presence. In these moments, there is an innate care and security present. Technological contact is a great output, but when it is over, there is a void for human connection and the energy and feelings when people speak heart-to heart.

Certainly, with technology, information and data are available to help understand events and circumstances. However, a simple contact via phone or technology is void of the very important need to be physically present with friends or family. Being in each other's presence develops one of those memorable moments that is remembered throughout life. Those moments are defining because of the emotional and mindful ties developed between two people.

In many ways, these defining moments occur because of the rudimentary emotional and intuitive need people have for each other—understanding, closeness, and love. These moments of truth are decisive and remembered because of sincere communication. Their emotional, intellectual, and spiritual connection is created through verbal and nonverbal communication where people are authentically present and at hand.

Defining moments involve being with others in a genuine and true manner. No role-playing. No power trips. Just being in the moment without other thoughts or desires evident. Simply, being authentic and letting verbal and silent energy flow between them. Any and all past feelings or allusions are swept away: just two people together, real and genuine. In these moments, individuals are unafraid to reveal themselves, which is a true, trustworthy, and noble gesture.

In these times, a conscious sense of wisdom is present. Clarity and understanding of the nature and importance of relationships become clear and cherished. Moments such as these do not follow a flowchart or recipe but evolve because of the honest emotional connection and energy between them.

Does wisdom just happen magically? There is an intellectual and emotional aspect of it. Communication is more than speech. Motives, feelings, and other intangibles are expressed verbally and nonverbally. In true relationships, communication is authentic.

LISTENING AND WISDOM

What does listening have to do with wisdom? Listening involves interpreting and understanding. But wisdom? Where does that fit in? Is it a topic of discussion? Or is there more? Is wisdom a result of listening and complex thinking?

People do not sit down and say, "Let's have a conversation about wisdom." It may happen in philosophy classes or when making decisions, but generally, it does not appear to be a regular topic of discussion.

People equate conversations with knowledge and information. When they interact, they generally share facts, experiences, and, sometimes, data. The purpose is for people to be aware and cognizant of issues, research, observations, or news. Sharing what is happening, or simply staying connected, is what most conversations are about.

It is possible that some discussions, lectures, or presentations provide not only knowledge but also ignite insight, which is deeper than simply understanding facts. Insight speaks to how things occur and fit together and the meaning of knowledge and values. People with insight on the subject know more than simple facts and comprehend the context and the possibilities of that knowledge.

Wisdom involves both knowledge and insight, which are important in evaluating and understanding their application of both to life and circumstances. Wisdom determines and uncovers what is truthful and is in harmony with values and principles through reason and analysis. It concerns why things are as they are, and their meaning and influences in relationships and life.

Listening is affected by one's philosophy. Discussions and conversations frequently involve problem identification, potential solutions, and the wisdom of what is correct and ethical. Basically, individuals have to determine philosophically and practically whether or not standards, ethics, and decisions were prudent and relevant for the organization and people. The focus is on philosophical or procedural ideas or matters.

Finding personal or organizational wisdom is difficult: some do not even think about it. American culture is absorbed with pragmatic work and distraction. People become filled with themselves and their own needs and do not look inward to examine their behavior and its impact and appropriateness. Nor do they look externally and evaluate their impact on others and determine its depth and thoughtfulness.

In many situations, an employer, friend, or relative will say, "What's on your mind?" In most cases, they wonder where the person is emotionally and intellectually: they want to know and understand what people think and their reasoning.

Intellectual conversations reveal cognitive or academic matters, but they do not necessarily touch the reality of the inner person. They generally explore what and how people think about circumstances and engage in the possibility of problem-solving. Exploring and questioning ideas and concepts—what they are and their impact—is an integral part of cognitive conversations, in which information and logic are important to discern the validity of the various points of view.

Being mindful is necessary in confirming the wisdom of individual or group decisions. To do so requires quiet reflection and even solitude to wisely examine oneself and reflect on consequences. Basically, examining two questions: Who am I? and Why am I here? The answers are deeper than physical or employment issues. They are quite philosophical and relate to how one lives life with values, honor, and wisdom.

Who an individual really is as a human being moves deeper beyond cognitive conversations, in the sense that it reveals more than the mind and analytical discourse. In personal conversations, people open their hearts and souls and reveal their inner thoughts and feelings. Sharing what one really believes is not always easy. There are risks. Trust is a major requirement.

Exploring desires and personal reflections come from the heart and soul in the sense that strongly held emotions and values are revealed and shared. Any violation of trust in these circumstances destroys a relationship and any form of further connection. Sharing who one really is deep inside is a true gift to another person. The understanding that results disclose who the person is and what they stand for. These moments rely on respect and mutual regard.

With an authentic bond and honest discussion, closer ties and true connections evolve. They are not debates or lectures—they are more substantial and personally revealing. People give a piece of themselves in these interactions: feelings, emotions, needs, and philosophy.

Listening has an inner-self characteristic to it because listeners are not blank pages. Individual life experiences influence how they hear and interpret messages. Listeners have to introspectively examine their own prejudices, mindset, and feelings. Willingness to listen requires willingness to self-evaluate and moves more closely into another person's life. They have to let go and not be locked into filtering everything through their own circumstances and concerns or ambitions or priorities.

LISTENING AND WISDOM

Listening carefully and properly is necessary if the conversation is going to move from a simple exchange of information. It has to progress to a new and insightful level beyond shallow conversation about routine or trivial matters.

In retrospect, some conversations go to a different tier because of the behavior of the participants. These conversations move to examine choices and decisions. After all, decisions are judged based on their soundness and impact. Sound judgments are considered wise based on philosophical and ethical principles. Knowledge and certainly experience also go into making them.

Wisdom is not solely dependent on experience; it is also derived from reflecting thoughtfully and reviewing major lessons from those events[1]. Lessons learned are not always from textbooks. Clarity happens through thinking about events in defining what concepts, knowledge, and principles were important.

Some people perceive events through a black and white lens. Issues and answers seem clear. In major life circumstances, there are shades of gray and focus. Things are not always clear, and every decision has upsides and downsides, as well as timing. Deferring or quickly pushing decisions can have consequential effects in terms of being completed at the most beneficial time, or they can be "too much too soon" or "a day late and a buck short."

In addition, times and circumstances require the ability to challenge established conditions and processing. Knowing when to go against the grain or not do the expected may be needed at times. Better approaches may be necessary than simply following the established procedures or not doing the expected and looking outside the box. The status quo may have created a dilemma or problem. Moving away from it may be the best course.

Leaders and many others are quick to judge. Slicing and sorting approaches into good or bad categories can be overly simplistic. Understanding is necessary. Trying to comprehend the conditions and the perspective of others confronting them is important. Comprehending what made them act the way they did enables their perspective. Then, learning can take place and better advice to others to make more effective decisions in the future is possible.

HUMILITY

Successful leaders are not egocentric. They analyze, evaluate, and synthesize events and issues in order to find ways to address them. They realize that sometimes pain and failure are part of life. Success and failure both form the basis for personal growth and the prospect of finding greater wisdom.

Indian philosopher Jiddu Krishnamurti asserted that listening is an act of humility not of judgment or self-importance. He believed that most people do not really listen because they are distracted by the environment and certainly by their prejudices and biases. Internal personal barriers and attitudes can constrain listening. But removing them can open the person to true listening. Individuals do not have to like or agree with what they hear, but they can still understand the other person and their perception of circumstances and outcomes.

Krishnamurti stated,

> That very act of listening is humility. There is no effort involved, the mind has done nothing to be humble; it is humble, therefore it is capable of listening. . . . Because I want to understand what another is talking about, I am not offering my opinion, my objections, my arguments; that is all laid aside, and I listen to what is being said. That very listening is humility; the mind is humble in that very act; therefore there is no effort to be humble. The arrogant mind cannot listen. The mind that is full of knowledge, argumentation, that has acquired, experienced—such a mind is incapable of listening, because it is full of vanity, conceit. So the problem is not how to get rid of conceit, but whether the mind is able to listen. When it can listen, the mind is in a state of humility, and then it is capable of perceiving totally, from which action follows.[2]

Having one's story truly heard connects people together in the present and the future. True discourse involves an emotional attachment and understanding.

THE ART OF LISTENING

Ursula La Guin stated emphatically that listening is not a mechanistic, machine-like activity: it is not simply stimulus-response. In a continuous interchange between two people, their consciousness goes both ways all the time. "Listening is not a reaction, it is a connection. Listening to a conversation or a story, we don't so much respond as join in—become part of the action."[3] People get in tune with each other. The listener's listening enables the speaker's speaking.

To be an artful listener, Erich Fromm[4] indicates there are certain norms and guidelines. Obviously, the complete concentration of the listener is fundamental. Nothing, including anxiety or self-interest, must be on his or her mind. Listening cannot be effective if the person's thoughts are distracting. However, a "free-working" imagination is helpful if it is "concrete to be expressed in words."

Empathy is essential in order to feel the experience of the other person as if they, themselves, experienced it. Love is a part of understanding. Not love in a romantic sense, but as an aspect of empathy and reaching out to another person. Understanding and loving are linked and inseparable; otherwise, the door to understanding is closed.

When truly listening, individuals demonstrate respect, let go, and allow themselves to be touched. Emotions are also a part of listening, particularly the passion, fire, fear, or soft-heartedness they feel. Listeners do not have to prepare their responses. They just have to listen and react naturally and authentically. Listeners put the other person before themselves and open themselves to them and their philosophy.

While incarcerated by the Nazis, which resulted in his death in 1945, Dietrich Bonhoeffer wrote to a friend, Eberhard Bethge, about the personal importance of discussion. He missed these conversations greatly and the need for friends and others. He wrote this to Bethge about wishing he could have a discussion with him over his recent writing about the life of a middle-class family—about the importance of conversation with friends.

He stated,

> You would recognize many familiar features, and you come into it too. But I haven't yet got much further than the beginning, mainly because the repeated false forecasts of my release have made it difficult for me to concentrate. But the work is giving me great pleasure. Only I wish I could talk it over with you every day; indeed, I miss that more than you think. I may often have originated our ideas, but the clarification of them was completely on your side. I only learnt in conversation with you whether an idea was any good or not. I long to read to you some of what I've written. Your comments on details are so much better than mine. Perhaps that seems to be mad presumption?![5]

Bonhoeffer's letter details the value of discussions face-to-face with his friend to garner his perspective and interpretation. The mind, according to him, requires discussion. Wisdom emerges from thought, and conversation provides a perspective and insight from others. Shared wisdom is a genuine gift.

Wisdom is not the regurgitation of facts and is not a competitive activity. While wise people may have a broad and deep background and information and knowledge, there is a distinction between being smart and being wise. Wisdom is more difficult to acquire than encyclopedic knowledge, and it is more than a cognitive exercise.

Wisdom includes the ability to empathize with others, which involves listening and deep understanding of people, events, and outcomes. Being aware of other people's experiences and life is a part of listening wisely. Sensitivity to the growth of others in an empathic way creates trust and a deeper connection.

Wisdom is also comprehending that uncertainty will always exist in life. Interpretations are evident in an individual's comments, attitudes, and perspectives. Common sense and intelligence get to the core of issues, and their contexts are also important.

A major aspect is moral discernment and emotional intelligence to understand and act with justice and values. Understanding philosophy is important in discussing absolutes and approaches to life. Acting and validating the moral imperatives involved ensures that behavior and values are consistently applied and enforced. Moral principles and judgment are essential for wise decisions and behavior—they are necessary for everyday life.

Wisdom grows out of the heart and the intellect. A big difference exists between being schooled and being educated. There are many historical examples of people who had impressive academic credentials who acted in uncivilized and brutish ways. And there are many examples of people, without formal training or education, who acted with wisdom and compassion.

Wisdom has several dimensions: cognitive, virtue, and goodness.[6] Cognitive processes include attaining and addressing information. However, the core concerns enduring truths and the hierarchical ordering of values and actions directed at those truths. Wisdom is essential when circumstances require judgments in uncertain and evolving situations and times. Wisdom as a virtue concerns ascertaining the consequences of events to determine the best "supreme good." This creates the way for moral action and virtuous decisions.

Finally, wisdom is a personal good that provides the best out of life. Self-reflection and growth are integral parts of pursuing wisdom. Intrinsic rewards come through finding meaning and living based on principles and moral values. Wisdom involves creativity, curiosity, learning, and mastering knowledge and skills, but also perspective and understanding of the world and the implication of decisions. Courage, integrity, and perseverance are necessary for wisdom in life's decisions. Justice and humanity are basic principles that lead to a "good" society.

Wisdom requires intelligence and exemplary judgment, taking stock of events, listening to others, and determining what actions are morally valued, enhance humanity, and provide insight into ideas, motives, and behavior.

Ethical conduct and behavior are based on clear and strong values and principles.

Self-knowledge and reflection are necessary, as is holding oneself up to principles. Experience and reflective thinking open the opportunity for new ways of thinking. A sense of the common good, as well as understanding the motives of others, not merely judging them, is essential in making wise decisions. Wisdom uncovers the positive and negative unconscious forces that operate silently and powerfully to affect perception, feelings, thinking, and actions.

Wisdom and honor go hand-in-hand. People's values and actions are honest, fair, and worthy of respect. Being respectful and trustworthy are qualities of honorable individuals because they are reliable and mean what they say and follow through.

Honor is a moral imperative based on acting with integrity and honesty. Certainly, listening and thinking are attributes in building positive and constructive relationships with others. Authenticity, following through, compassion, clear values, and truth are qualities of honorable people. They also demonstrate honor and respect to truly listen to others as they speak their mind and reveal their inner thoughts and feelings.

NOTES

1. Adam Grant, "How to Think Like a Wise Person," *Psychology Today*, 2013.

2. Jiddu Krishnamurti, "Bombay 5th Public Talk," March 18, 1956, https://jkrishnamurti.org/content/bombay-5th-public-talk-18th-march-1956/Listening.

3. Ursula K. Le Guin, *The Wave in the Mind: Talks and Essays on the Writer, the Reader, and the Imagination* (Shambhala, 2004), 196, Kindle.

4. Fromm, *The Art of Listening*, 192, Kindle.

5. Bonhoeffer Dietrich, *Letters & Papers from Prison* (New York: Touchstone Books, 1971), 130.

6. Robert J. Sternberg, *Wisdom: It's Nature, Origins, and Development* (New York: Cambridge University Press, 1990), 28–36.

Bibliography

Adler, Mortimer J. *How to Speak—How to Listen*. Touchstone, 1997a.

Adler, Mortimer J. *Ten Philosophical Mistakes*. Touchstone, 1997b.

Arendt, Hannah. *Crises of the Republic: Lying in Politics, Civil Disobedience, Nonviolence, Thoughts on Politics and Revolution*. Houghton Mifflin Harcourt, 1972.

Arendt, Hannah. *The Origins of Totalitarianism*. Harvest Books, 1973.

Arendt, Hannah. *Eichmann in Jerusalem: A Report on the Banality of Evil*. Penguin Publishing Group, 2006.

Bickford, Susan. *Dissonance of Democracy*. New York: Cornell University Press, 1996.

Bohm, David. *Thought as a System*. Taylor and Francis, 2004.

Bohm, David. *On Dialogue*. Taylor and Francis, 2012.

Bonhoeffer, Dietrich. *Letters & Papers from Prison*. New York: Touchstone Books, 1971.

Cousins, Norman. *Human Options*. New York: W. W. Norton and Company, 1981.

Dobson, Andrew. *Listening for Democracy*. Oxford University Press, 2014.

Dweck, Carol S. *Mindset*. New York: Ballantine Books, 2008.

Ellinor, Linda, and Gerard, Glenna. *Dialogue: Rediscover the Transforming Power of Conversation*. Crossroad Press, 2014.

Fromm, Erich. *The Art of Listening*. Open Road Media, 2013.

Gardner, Howard. *Frames of Mind*. New York: Basic Books, 1993.

Gardner, Howard. *Five Minds of the Future*. Boston: Harvard Business Press, 2008.

Goens, George A. *Soft Leadership for Hard Times*. Lanham, MD: Rowman & Littlefield, 2005.

Goens, George A. *Civility Lost: The Media, Politics, and Education*, Lanham, MD: Rowman and Littlefield, 2019a.

Goens, George A. *The Person in the Mirror*. Lanham, MD: Rowman and Littlefield, 2019b.

Greenspan, Miriam. *Healing Through the Dark Emotions*. Boston: Shambala Publications, 2003.

Hall, Edith. *Aristotle's Way: How Ancient Wisdom Can Change Your Life*. Penguin Publishing Group, 2019.

Isaacs, William. *Dialogue and the Art of Thinking Together*. New York: Currency Publishers, 1999.

Jacoby, Susan. *The Age of American Unreason*. New York: Vintage Books, 2009.

Johannsen, Richard L., Valde, Kathleen S., and Whedbee, Karen E. *Ethics in Human Communication*. Waveland Press, Inc., 2007.

Kahane, Adam. *Collaborating with the Enemy: How to Work with People You Don't Agree with or Like or Trust*. Berrett-Koehler Publishers, 2017.

Kofman, Fred. *The Meaning Revolution: The Power of Transcendent Leadership*. The Crown Publishing Group, 2018.

LeGuin, Ursula K. *The Wave in the Mind: Talks and Essays on the Writer, the Reader, and the Imagination*. Shambhala, 2004.

Levin, Yuval. *The Fractured Republic*. New York: Basic Books, 2016.

Lipari, Lisbeth. *Listening, Thinking, Being*. University Park, Pennsylvania: Pennsylvania State University Press, 2014.

Maslow, Abraham. *The Psychology of Science*. New York: Harper and Row, 1996.

Moldoveanu, Mihnea, and Martin, Roger. *Diaminds: Decoding the Mental Habits of Successful Thinkers*. Toronto: University of Toronto Press, 2010.

O'Donohue, John. *Eternal Echoes*. New York: Cliff Street Books, 1999.

Rogers, Carl R., and Farson, Richard E. *Active Listening*. Mansfield Centre, CT: Martino Publishing, 2015.

Scalia, Antonin, and Gardner, Bryan A. *Making Your Case*. St. Paul, MN: Thompson/West, 2008.

Scharmer, Otto, and Kaufer, Katrin. *Leading from the Emerging Future: From Ego-System to Eco-System Economies*. Barrett-Kohler Publishers, 2013.

Schein, Edgar H. *Humble Inquiry: The Gentle Art of Asking Instead of Telling*. Barrett-Koehler Publishers, 2013.

Senge, Peter M., et al. *Presence: An Exploration of Profound Change in People, Organizations, and Society*. The Crown Publishing Group, 2005.

Sternberg, Robert J. *Wisdom: It's Nature, Origins, and Development*. New York: Cambridge University Press, 1990.

Strossen, Nadine. *HATE: Why We Should Resist It with Free Speech, Not Censorship*. Oxford University Press, 2018.

White, E. B. *On Democracy*. New York: HarperCollins, 2019.

Whyte, David. *The Heart Aroused*. New York: Currency Doubleday, 1994.

Whyte, David. *Consolations: The Solace, Nourishment and Underlying Meaning of Everyday Words*. Langley, Washington: Many Rivers Press, 2015.

PERIODICAL, BLOGS, REPORTS

Akst, Daniel. "The Reopening of the Liberal Mind," *Wall Street Journal*, May 24, 2019.

Blue Cross Blue Shield. "Major Depression: Impact on Overall Health," May 10, 2018.

Brodie, Graham D. "Issues in the Measurement of Listening," *Communication Research Reports*, Vol. 30. No. 1, January–March, 2013.

Brooks, David. "When Trolls and Crybullies Rule the Earth," *New Times*, May 5, 2019.

Business Insider. "Christopher Nolan Explains the Audio Illusion that Created the Unique Music in Dunkirk," July 24, 2017.

Carlin, George. "Something to Ponder," *The Medium*, January 1, 2018.

Elder, Linda. "Become a Critical Thinker," The Head of the Foundation for Critical Thinking. *The Necessary Revolution in the Way We Think*. http://www.forbesindia .com/interview/rotman/become-a-critical-thinker/26592/1.

Grant, Adam. "How to Think Like a Wise Person," *Psychology Today*, 2013.

Healy, Thomas. "Who's Afraid of Free Speech?" *The Atlantic*, June 2017.

Howick Associates. "Listening Statistics," https://b2b.kununu.com/blog/ why-do-good-employees-quit-leave-their-job.

John Paul Stevens, Speech delivered by Supreme Court Justice. "The Freedom of Speech," *Yale Law School*, October 27, 1992.

Krishnamurti, Jiddu. "Bombay 5th Public Talk," March 18, 1956. https:// jkrishnamurti.org/content/bombay-5th-public-talk-18th-march-1956/Listening.

Maslow, Abraham H. "A Theory of Human Motivation," *Psychology Classics*, 1943. www.all-about-psychology.com.

McNamara, Jim. "The Lost Art of listening," Public Lecture, *London School of Economics*, November 23, 2016.

Mill, John Stewart. "On Liberty," *Stanford Encyclopedia of Philosophy*. https://plato .stanford.edu/entries/mill/.

NPR. "It's Been a Minute with Sam Saunders, Free Speech vs. Hate Speech," https:// www.npr.org/templates/transcript/transcript.php?storyId=616085863.

Obama, Barack. "Remarks: Memorial Service: Tucson," https://obamawhitehouse .archives.gov/the-press-office/2011/01/12/remarks-president-barack-obama-memorial-service-victims-shooting-tucson.

Perrin, Andrew. "10 Facts About Smart Phones as the iPhone Turns 10," *PEW*, June 28, 2017.

Popova, Maria. "Albert Camus on Consciousness and the Lacuna Between Truth and Meaning," *Brain Pickings*, December 26, 2016.

Prysbylski, Andrew K., and Weinstein, Netta. "Can You Connect with Me Now? How the Presence of Mobile Communication Technology Influences Face-to-Face Conversation Quality," *Journal of Social and Personal Relationships*, July 19, 2012.

Publishing Services-University of Minnesota Libraries. "Business Communication for Success," 2015.

Quinnipiac University Poll. "Deep Dissatisfaction Among U.S. Voters," https://poll .qu.edu/national/release-detail?ReleaseID=2340.

Sartwll, Crispin. "Hatred Enhances Your Self-Esteem," *Walt Street Journal*, July 1, 2019.

Schein, Edgar H. "Dialogue, Culture, and Organizational Learning," *Reflections*, 2003. Vol. 4, No. 4. pp. 27–38.

Seltzer, Leon F. "Feeling Understood – Even More Important Than Feeling Loved," *Psychology Today*, June 28, 2017.

The Ethics Centre. "Ethics Explainer: Freedom of Speech," February 22, 2017. https://ethics.org.au/ethics-explainer-freedom-of-speech/.

The Fire. "Hate Speech," March 29, 2019. https://thefire.org/issues/hate-speech/.

Thomas, Evan. "Sandra Day O'Connor's Lessons in Leadership," *Wall Street Journal*, March 7, 2019.

Topornycky, Joseph, and Golparian, Shaya. "Building Openness and Interpretation in Active Listening," *Collective Essays on Learning and Teaching (CELT)*, Vol. IX, 2016.

Twenge, Jean M. "Have Smartphones Destroyed a Generation?" *The Atlantic*, September 2017.

United States Supreme Court. "Snyder v. Philips et al. October Term," 2010. https://www.supremecourt.gov/opinions/10pdf/09-751.pdf.

Wermiel, Stephen. "The Ongoing Challenge to Define Free Speech," *American Bar Association.*

Wiesel, Elie. "The Perils of Indifference," https://americanrhetoric.com/speeches/ewieselperilsofindifference.html.

Wiesel, Ellie. "One Must Not Forget," *US News and World Report*, October 27, 1986.

Index

About the Author

George A. Goens, PhD, has written seven books and coauthored four others on leadership, school reform, education, and social issues. He served as a school district executive and in graduate teaching positions, as well as a leadership consultant to public boards and professional leaders.

www.ingramcontent.com/pod-product-compliance
Lightning Source LLC
Chambersburg PA
CBHW020357100426
42812CB00001B/89